Karl Vaters

The Grasshopper Myth

Big Churches, Small Churches and the Small Thinking that Divides Us

NewSmallChurch.com

The Grasshopper Myth: Big Churches, Small Churches and the
Small Thinking that Divides Us
Copyright 2012 by Karl Vaters

Published by New Small Church
NewSmallChurch.com

Cover Design: Concept by: Karl Vaters
                     Graphic Design by: TaylorPfeifer.com

Cover Photos: Grasshopper/Katydid photo by Vitali Dyatchenko.
                     Licensed through iStock.com.
                     Back cover author photo by George Sam Beaver

Typesetting by: CJ Media, Montclair, California
Printed by: New Song Media - brad@newsongmedia.com
Second printing: 2013
Printed in the United States of America

ISBN: 978-0-9884439-0-7
Religion / Christian Ministry / Pastoral Resources

To Shelley,

For loving Jesus

Speaking the truth

And inspiring me

The Grasshopper Myth

Definition: The false impression that our Small Church ministry is less than what God says it is because we compare ourselves with others.

Origin: The Hebrews at the edge of the Promised Land.

> *All the people we saw there are of great size. ...We seemed like grasshoppers in our own eyes, and we looked the same to them.*
> *— Numbers 13:32-33*

Symptoms: Lack of vision, faith, courage, effectiveness and freedom.

Prognosis: A lifetime of wandering, whining and placing blame. And yes, it is contagious.

Treatment: There's a New Small Church in town – a place of hope and healing.

We've discovered the benefits of thinking small. And it's got nothing to do with small thinking.

We've come to realize that our small size is not a problem to be fixed, but a strategic advantage God wants to use.

We're heading out with vision, faith and courage into places God wants us to go. Places giants cannot tread.

Chapters

I wish someone else had written this book.

Thirty years ago.

Reading it back then would have saved me a lot of grief.

I looked for a book like it for years.

Then I realized that if I wanted to read it, I'd have to write it.

My prayer is that it may do for you what it wasn't able to do for me.

Because it didn't exist when I needed it most.

—Karl Vaters

Chapter 1

Hi, I'm Karl and I'm a Small Church Pastor

If the title of this chapter sounds like an Alcoholics Anonymous introduction, you've got the right idea.

I am a Small Church pastor.

And I am not a failure.

It's taken me almost thirty years in pastoral ministry to write those last two sentences. Now that I've been able to write them, I know I'm finally entering a life of recovery from The Grasshopper Myth.

I Am a Small Church Pastor

I have been the lead pastor of three churches in the last 25 years. More than twenty years in my current congregation. Those churches were very different from each other in almost every way, except one.

They were all Small Churches.

Yet despite two-and-a-half decades in Small Church ministry I didn't believe I was a Small Church pastor until very recently. I had convinced myself I was a big church pastor stuck in a Small Church building.

That's where The Grasshopper Myth begins. At least it's where it began for me.

I believed the myth so badly that I soon came to hate the small church building for what it was doing to me – how it was stifling my ministry.

Soon I started to hate myself for not being able to grow a big church.

Then I started hating the ministry.

Eventually I felt myself starting to hate God for leading me on, only to let me down.

I have no one but myself to blame for those feelings, but they didn't come out of thin air. Eleanor Roosevelt is credited with saying, "No one can make you feel inferior without your consent." Over the past thirty-plus years I gave that consent to people who don't even know me and who had no idea I was misusing their attempts to help me.

If you're in pastoral ministry, this is not the first book you've read on pastoring. You've probably read many of the same books and attended the same conferences I have. You know the ones I'm talking about. A pastor goes to an existing church or starts a new one, and within a surprisingly short period of time the church grows, its ministries expand and the pastor makes a name for him or herself.

Other pastors start wondering how that pastor did it, so eager ministers are invited to hear how it was done. Other successful pastors are brought in to co-teach the conference, and the struggling pastors sit in hopeful anticipation as successful pastors share their stories and strategies.

I've been one of those struggling pastors. I still am in many ways. And I've received some very helpful ideas from those conferences and books.

Years ago, when I started attending them, the leaders in my church always knew when I'd been to one because I'd come home all revved up about the latest idea, convinced this was the key to getting our church to the next level.

Sometimes I'd take the principles I'd learned and re-teach them to my staff and volunteers. If a book was particularly good I'd make it required reading for them, then we'd gather and talk about it. Some church leaders would catch the same vision I had caught, but some would drag their heels.

The conference had told us about the heel-draggers, so I was prepared. They were the Problem People, the Vision-Killers, the We've-Never-Done-It-That-Way-Before crowd. I was not going to let them get me down as I boldly stepped out in this fresh, new way of doing church.

But somehow, I could never duplicate the success of the pastor who gave the seminar or wrote the book. After a few months of excitement, energy and expense, one or two ideas would make their way into our church's culture, but most would fade away from lack of interest. The book with all the answers would drift from my desk to my shelf to my closet and I would quietly blame the Heel-Draggers for killing God's vision.

Over the years I found it more cost-effective to read more books and go to fewer seminars, but even the book-reading waned as the pattern repeated itself. The conferences and books were more likely to leave me discouraged and frustrated than excited and motivated.

So I quit.

For several years I stopped going to seminars and reading ministry books. I went to movies and read novels instead. It was a nice break from the pressure to perform, because when Will Smith saved the world he didn't expect me to go home and do it too.

What was wrong with me? I would ask. I'm a bright person. I know I'm called to pastoral ministry. I know I'm called to pastor this specific church.

Why can't I make it what it's supposed to be?

Why won't it *grow*?!

It wasn't the fault of the seminars, the books or the pastors. Their successes made me feel inferior because I gave them consent by comparing myself to them. The more I admired them and tried to duplicate their success, the more I felt like the ten faithless Hebrew spies. The megachurch pastors looked like giants, the giants felt like enemies, and I seemed like a grasshopper *in my own eyes*.

The megachurch pastors who wrote the books and taught the seminars never intended to do that to me. They were trying to use their successes as a tool to help me. I was the one who turned it as a weapon against myself. And it all happened based on my failure to recognize one essential characteristic of my ministry identity.

I'm a Small Church pastor.

The first time I admitted that truth to myself was one of the most liberating moments of my life. As soon as I recognized it, I was OK with it. The more I became OK with, the better I did it. I finally knew who I was and how God made me to minister. I was free from the burden of trying to become someone I was never meant to be.

And I Am Not a Failure

If my church is small, how can I call myself, my church or my ministry a success?

How can I even call the church healthy?

Don't all healthy things grow?

Yes they do. The problem is that too many of us have defined church success and health by numbers. And not just by any numbers. By two specific numbers. Butts in the seats and bucks in the offering.

? does that guarantee a healthy church

The higher the better.

This obsession with numerical growth is not healthy.

Those who write the books and hold the seminars like to promote the success stories that result from their guidance, and understandably so. But pastors in my position see something they don't see – the casualties on the other side of the ledger.

This drive for greater numbers and larger churches has probably resulted in more pastoral burnout than healthy, growing churches. Not to mention the tens of thousands of confused and damaged church attenders whose opinions and needs were belittled and shoved aside for newer and bigger things. Many of them left their churches permanently and never went back to any church at all.

In the chapter *So What's Wrong With Church Growth?* I'll challenge the premise that biblical growth and health can be accurately measured by counting bodies. But for now let me ask a question many pastors never ask – I know I went many years without considering it.

What is biblical church growth?

Forget the numbers.

What does Jesus measure?

I fear that most pastors are like the child in the following true story.

I was in the church lobby after a Sunday service when a friend approached me with a smile. "You're not going to believe what Lauren told me yesterday", she said. "She was going on about how she couldn't wait to grow up because she wanted to be bigger. She's at the age where she thinks the older you get the bigger you get, and she can't wrap her mind around the idea that her grandmother is older than me, since Grandma's so tiny."

I smiled, remembering when my own kids were that small and naïve.

The mom continued. "So there we were chatting about this, when all of a sudden, Lauren looked up at me and gasped 'Mom! Pastor Karl must be the oldest person in the whole wide world!'"

I roared with laughter. At 6'6", I was the tallest person six-year-old Lauren had ever met.

Yes, all healthy things grow. But growth is never as simple as *older equals taller* or *healthy equals bigger*. A pea will never be the size of a pumpkin and a rose won't ever reach the height of a redwood no matter how much you water them, fertilize them or teach them redwood growth principles. It's just not in their nature. All healthy, living things reach their optimal size at maturity, then they grow in different ways from that point on. What ways?

What if that principle applied to churches? I have come to believe it does. If the church is one body with many parts, isn't it possible, even likely, that the body of Christ needs churches of all sizes?

I am not a failure if my church reaches its optimal stage of maturity, then starts growing in ways other than butts in seats for weekend services. In fact it is essential that a church grow in other ways than its size if it is to take the next critical step in true church growth – from being healthy to being health*ful*.

There is a difference between healthy and healthful. And that difference matters.

We went through years of struggles after I arrived at my current church. They'd had several short-term pastorates before me, and it had taken a toll. But eventually we arrived at a place where we knew the church was finally healthy for the first time in a decade or more.

Then one day I was sitting behind the wheel of my car in the church parking lot and I asked myself, "now what?" I'd spent almost four years helping this Small Church get over some bad history, and now it was healthy.

What do you do with a healthy church?

As I sat in my car I realized that the leadership and I had just spent years under the hood of our church, tinkering with all the mechanical problems, and now here I was sitting in the driver's seat of a healthy church – and I had *no idea* where to take it!

The answer? Healthy things need to become health*ful* things.

Healthy plants take in the proper nutrients and grow strong, but if they provide no value to anyone outside themselves they're not health*ful*. A healthful plant is not just healthy, but is also supplying valuable fruit to others. For example there are healthy mushrooms that are healthful to humans and healthy mushrooms that are poisonous, and therefore not healthful to us at all.

The body of Christ needs to be more conscious of what healthful growth looks like. In fact, a church can't truly call itself healthy until it is healthful as well. And in Small Churches that awareness has to start with pastors being OK with who God has called us to be and what he has called us to do.

As I sat in the car that day, that's what I realized. The next step was to take our healthy church and make it a healthful one for others to gain nourishment from. Not because we needed greater numbers, but because our community needed greater hope.

Optimal church size is a topic we'll take a closer look at in the chapter *God Doesn't Take Attendance*.

Recovering from The Grasshopper Myth

Are Small Churches nothing more than places that failed at being big churches?

Are we destined to spend our ministry lives in the massive shadows cast by the big churches that dominate the landscape?

Or are we something more?

Certainly there are many failing churches of all styles and sizes, but size alone is not enough evidence to determine failure or success.

I propose that the following is true about the New Small Church

We are not sick
We are not failing
We are not stuck
We are not incompetent
We are not limited in our vision
We do not need to be fixed
We are not *less* than...

We are God's idea.

We are small.

Because we are small we have blessings to offer the body of Christ, our communities, our cities, our nations and our world that no one else can offer in quite the way we can.

Joel Osteen couldn't do my job.

That's no slam on him. I couldn't pastor Lakewood Church. And that's no slam on me. Brian Houston and Craig Groeschel couldn't do my job either. They're just not wired that way.

If a guy like Brian Houston came to Fountain Valley, there's no question he'd succeed in building a big church. In a few months he'd have found a bigger building to host the growing crowds and all the new ministries. Undoubtedly it would be a good church too – with awesome worship. But it wouldn't be the same church anymore. In order for it to work for him, it would have to become a very different church than it is now. Some things would be gained by that, but some really good things would be lost too.

This is not to say that the successes of these megachurch pastors came easily. I know they have all been through hard-fought battles. But they succeeded. And the evidence of their success is obvious. However, what would be lost by turning my church into a megachurch would be less obvious, just as the successes of my church right now are less obvious.

I'm not alone. There are a lot of great churches which just happen to be small. But we can't reach our full effectiveness until we accept our God-given place in the body of Christ and redirect our resources from a false model of numerical growth to a more biblical model.

People choose to attend Small Churches, not in spite of their size, but because of it. Pastors of the New Small Church are the ones who have accepted that and celebrate it. We've stopped whining about the problems and challenges that come with smallness and have embraced the strengths and opportunities. In doing that, we've finally caught up to what most of our congregation members have known all along – there's a lot to love about a dynamic Small Church.

Small Churches have been and will likely always be how most people choose to receive the bulk of their spiritual nourishment. We need to quit telling them they're shopping at the wrong store.

My Prayer for You, the Reader

What I have written in the following pages comes from hope.

After years of unnecessary frustration in pastoral ministry I have discovered emotional and spiritual healing by accepting how God made me. If what I've written can help anyone else avoid or defeat similar frustrations, I will have succeeded.

So, as you read this, I pray...

... that other Small Church pastors won't have to suffer the (self-inflicted) grief I have suffered.

... that New Small Churches and their pastors will not just see their *future* potential (as in, when they become a big church), but realize their God-given value *at the size they are right now*. They may even stay that size because that may be God's will for them.

... that medium, to big, to megachurches and their pastors will join hands and hearts with their New Small Church counterparts to teach and to learn from each other.

... that we can encourage and be encouraged by each other, valuing every church's unique contributions to the kingdom of God, "...that there should be no division in the body, but that its parts should have equal concern for each other."

... that bible schools, seminaries, pastoral conferences, publishers and denominations will start using the wisdom and experiences of New Small Church pastors to help train the current and next generation of pastors – 80% of whom will never lead a church of more than 200 people – to appreciate, utilize and develop the distinct skill-sets required for different church sizes.

... that church statisticians will find a way to redefine church growth as more than the number of people in the seats for weekend services to the exclusion of almost all other factors.

... that when pastors ask each other, "so how's your church going?" we will talk about life transformation first and attendance figures last – if at all. That we will share personal stories rather than offering-basket figures. That we will <u>burst with passion</u> for the people in our churches and communities more than our facility expansion plans.

... that my fellow New Small Church pastors will be released from the guilt, stress, and feelings of inferiority that come with trying to live up to an unbiblical ideal. That they will find renewed hope, encouragement and passion for their congregations whose names and faces they know and whose lives they share.

... that The Grasshopper Myth will be diagnosed so that it can be seen for what it is – a myth, a delusion, a mirage, a false self. A lie.

... that the body of Christ will unite to defeat this lie and will find a way to utilize all its parts, large and small, to <u>experience the joy of worship</u>, the <u>healing power of fellowship</u> and <u>have a greater, more biblical impact on the world.</u> *or community*

These are lofty goals for a first book from a pastor whose church building is small enough to be invisible to 90% of the people who drive past it every day. I have no illusions that it will accomplish all, or even most of that.

But I hope to get a conversation started.

Chapter 2

How Trying to Build a Big Church Nearly Killed Me — and My Church

My story is my story. I have debated including it here because it is so singular and personal.

Plus, this is not an autobiography, with good reason. My life story is neither heroic enough nor horrific enough to get anyone's adrenaline rushing. I have nothing to whine about or boast about.

Yet I'm also aware that the most personal stories can be the most universal. So I welcome you to take anything from my life that can help you walk through your life.

The Church Kid Grows Up

I am a third generation pastor, raised in a great home by parents who loved God, served the church and put their family first.

My father's father spent almost his entire ministry as a national church official, yet no one ever referred to him by any title but

Pastor Vaters. A pastor to other pastors. His wife, my grandmother, was the preacher of the family, known for weaving great anecdotes in the pulpit, only to provide a twist at the end that would leave people wanting more.

I came to know Christ when I was six or seven. While the adults were having evangelistic meetings in the sanctuary of the Stone Church in Toronto, Canada, my father had made sure the kids in the basement got more than baby-sitting. We were delighted every evening with Bible lessons told through magic-tricks with colored handkerchiefs and rabbit-out-of-the-hat illusions that made Bible lessons come alive.

Each night the magician/evangelist closed by asking if any children wanted to accept Jesus into their hearts and inevitably several did. About halfway through the week he told us that we weren't Christians just because our parents were. It was a decision we had to make for ourselves. Either he hadn't said that before or I hadn't heard it before. I heard it then.

I made my decision that night. And I've never turned back. Yes, I've had occasional times of doubt and uncertainty. I've even asked my share of hard questions, more in my adult years than in my childhood or youth, but I can truly say from that moment on I've lived as a follower of Jesus.

When I was 16, my dad took a trip to California. When he came back, he and my mom called me and my younger sisters into the living room to tell us that he felt called by God to move to Modesto to pastor a small church – much smaller than the one he was currently pastoring. He also told us that this was a family decision. My sisters and I were 16, 14 and 12 years of age and my dad knew that moving almost 3,000 miles to a different country wouldn't work well if we weren't all on board for it.

We looked outside the window. It was winter and we were being asked if we wanted to move from Canada to California. It didn't require a hard sell.

I graduated from high school shortly after the move, and found myself in junior college wondering what I would do with the rest of my life. I was sensing a call to ministry and fought against it for what seemed like an eternity, but was probably less than 18 months. I struggled because I knew the ministry was an individual calling and I wanted to be sure I wasn't going into it because it was the family business.

After giving in to God's call on my life, I spent the next two and a half years at Bethany Bible College. Upon graduation I had an Associate Pastor position waiting for me. That position was short-lived due to a pastoral change, and soon I was working on my father's pastoral staff as he transitioned into a new church in Silicon Valley.

On my first day at that church I met a beautiful redhead. One year later Shelley and I were married. Fourteen months after the wedding we were parents. Three years later, just before the birth of our second child, we left that fairly large church and moved to the Santa Cruz mountains where I became the Lead Pastor of a church with about thirty members in the tiny town of Felton.

The Church Growth Movement Moves Me

It was 1986, and the church growth movement was taking off. It was the topic of virtually every pastoral book, seminar and conference. Denominations started ambitious plans to apply church growth principles to launch new churches, equip struggling ones and increase the average church size.

Bible colleges had just begun teaching the church growth principles of Donald McGavran, C. Peter Wagner, Robert Schuller, *et al* when I was attending, but it kicked into high gear shortly after I graduated. By the time I was pastoring in Felton, church growth principles were accepted as *the* way *all* vital churches did things. I read and listened with growing excitement. Then I watched as many of my peers applied these principles and saw amazing success growing big- and megachurches (a new term and a relatively new idea at the time).

It was all so new. I spent the next several years unlearning most of what I'd been taught about how to do church. I'm still grateful that I did so. Not to be harsh on my college professors – they gave me a wonderful theological foundation – but the world was changing and most of their methodology had been expiring even as they were pouring it into my cup.

In the next few years, Shelley and I had our third and final child, followed by a short, miserable stint at a church in the northern end of the San Francisco Bay. Then we landed in Fountain Valley, just 8 miles south of Disneyland in December of 1992, where I became the pastor of Community Bible Church. I'll be saying more about the condition of the church in later chapters, but for now I'll tell you this; it was small, struggling and sickly, but the people who remained were not the cause of its problems. They were aware of the challenges and more than ready to step up to the task with a new and, as it turned out, shockingly naïve young pastor.

Driven to Do Something

Within a few months of arriving in Orange County my wife and I went on vacation to celebrate our 10th anniversary. While gone, we attended a Sunday service at a megachurch. What they had built and were about to build was impressive, especially since it was in a sparsely populated area. I introduced myself to the pastor and asked if I could buy him lunch the next day to pick his brain about pastoral ministry. He agreed and we had a nice lunch with him and his wife.

We told each other our stories and were both surprised to find that he had a history with the community we had just moved to, and knew more than I did about it. "It's a shame," he said about the church situation in the Fountain Valley area. "Nobody's doing anything there," by which he meant that, while Orange County has more than its share of megachurches, the immediate area where I was ministering had none.

That was all I needed. I flew from vacation determined that I would be the one who would finally "do something" in the Fountain Valley area.

For the next few years we worked to raise our family, pay the bills and build the church. But despite my best intentions, hard work and constant prayers the church only grew from small and struggling to slightly-less-small and slightly-less-struggling.

Then came *The Purpose Driven Church.*

Anyone who was a pastor in the late 1990s remembers the impact Rick Warren's book had on church leaders. It was nothing short of a world-wide phenomenon. And I was living less than a half-hour drive from the epicenter – Saddleback Church.

After reading the book, I bought copies for every church staff member and deacon. I made it required reading for them and their spouses, then I scheduled a Saturday strategy session to discuss its implications for our church.

When the church leaders walked in carrying dog-eared and highlighted copies of the book, they looked like they'd been hit by the same train that had run me over. They were as thrilled, scared, overwhelmed and enthused to enter this strange new world as I was. "We'll never go back to doing church the way we've done it" was one of the first comments when I opened the floor for feedback. We never did.

The following weekend we all drove to Lake Forest to take in a Saturday night service at Saddleback Church. It was impressive, encouraging, motivating and all kinds of intimidating.

Based on Purpose Driven principles, our church leadership team spent the next several months researching, planning, praying and laying out our own plan for transforming our little church into a Purpose Driven dynamo. The church members caught the excitement and we geared up for an Extreme Church Makeover.

After a months-long promotional campaign during which we canvassed the neighborhood to announce the coming of a "church for people who don't like church," we re-launched our church on October 1, 2000. Among other things, we added a second Sunday morning service (now with a coffee break in the middle of each), dropped the old hymns, stopped wearing suits and dresses, revamped the children's ministries curriculum, set up Rick Warren's baseball diamond discipleship strategy and changed the name of the church to Cornerstone Christian Fellowship.

And it worked! (Most of) the current members were excited about (most of) the changes and several families who'd never been to the church showed up and liked what they saw. For the next few years we rode a wave of excitement and growth until, on January 4, 2004 we moved our Sunday services to the auditorium of a local school, doubling our seating capacity. The move wasn't because we needed the space at the time, but because church growth principles told me to get more space *before* we needed it. We'd grown to just under 250 adults in a church sanctuary that holds a maximum of 350 (175 per service). In the school we'd be able to seat over 600 (300 per service) before we'd need a bigger space. I was sure we'd need to start looking very soon.

I felt like I was finally about to "do something".

Confusion and Confession

For just over a year an amazingly dedicated army of volunteers faithfully moved a church full of equipment into a school auditorium every Sunday, then packed it up and moved it back again. Sunday morning attendance grew in the new location right away and soon we were averaging almost 350 adults.

But the weekly grind started wearing on people, the metal folding chairs and lack of air-conditioning in the Jr High auditorium made the southern California summer services unendurable, and the lure of our own comfortable, cool, rent-free, chapel sitting empty started crying out to us. The crowds started dwindling. When the school couldn't rent to us anymore because of upcoming renovations, we took the shrinking congregation back to our old building in March 2005.

Everyone was thrilled to be back in a "real church".

I was miserable.

Going back seemed like going back*wards* and I felt like a failure.

Within six months my feelings of despair deepened as even more people left the church. I was convinced it was because we'd made this backwards move and no longer had the bigger room to inspire growth. The truth was that our shrinking congregation had more to do with the miserable mood the pastor was in. In spite of my best efforts to slap a smile on my face when I needed to, my emotional unrest was causing people to leave, which caused an even deeper melancholy inside me, which in turn caused greater unease, more departures, deeper depression...

I don't know how low the attendance fell in the next couple years. We were in free-fall and I stopped counting. Keeping track of attendance figures was great fun when we were growing, but it just made me miserable now. All I knew was we were fitting quite comfortably in our old, small church building again.

I was convinced I had been wronged somewhere along the way. After all, my desire to build a big church came from the right place. It had never been based on personal ambition. OK, that reared its ugly head on occasion, but it wasn't a driving factor. Now I felt like I was being punished as the unrighteous servant who had buried his talent in the ground even though I had tried *so hard* to invest it wisely.

I just wanted to be faithful to God. That's still all I want. And I was being told by the pastors I most admired that the best way to do that was to grow a big church. More people means more souls and more souls is what the kingdom of God is all about. Now it seemed like God had set me up for a task only to pull the goal out from under me when it was just about to happen.

Then I got angry. As I mentioned in the previous chapter, I started hating the church building. Feelings of rage would overwhelm me every time I drove up to it. Sometimes I would just keep driving, cancel my appointments with a lame excuse and go to a movie or to the beach where I'd sit and stare at the waves for hours. Aside from Shelley, I told none of this to anyone. I didn't even tell her a lot of it.

Eventually, I knew I needed help and sought out a counselor. Even that made me angry. Here I was providing pastoral counseling for free to people in my congregation – something I've always been pretty good at, even during this time – but when I needed the help I had to pay someone by the hour. Shortly after starting counseling I knew a weekly session wasn't going to be enough. I had to tell the people who loved me what was going on. Then I needed a break.

I started with my extended family. I told them what I was feeling and they were as loving as I knew they would be. Telling them was hard, but as soon as they knew, my burden felt a little lighter. They agreed that I was burned out and needed a break. And they started praying.

Because of their support, I was able to work up the nerve to tell my staff what was going on, followed by my deacon board. That was scary. I didn't know what their response would be, but if I was going to take a break from ministry they needed to know why. After all, without the deacons signing off on it and the staff agreeing to step up and cover my areas of ministry, I couldn't leave.

I didn't realize it at the time, but my entire future in ministry, including whether-or-not I would even *have* a future in ministry, hung on their response. At that point the deacon board had every right to tell me they would be looking for a new pastor. After all, the failure caused by the move to the school was my fault. The subsequent angst that was causing the current church exodus was because of me, too.

The response from both groups was a mixture of shock, sadness and relief. But mostly it was one of love. The relief they felt was because now a whole lot of things made sense to them. They'd seen the recent departures and they'd felt the same sense of unidentifiable unease.

Instead of judgment they gave me grace. When I told them I needed a break they only had one thing to say. "How long do you need?"

I will forever be in their debt.

I told them I needed forty days off. A good, biblical number. Eighty would have been better – twice as good, actually – but I didn't have the nerve to ask for that much. The forty days would start after the first Sunday of the new year.

Sunday, January 1, 2006 was the lowest moment of my ministerial life – and the day on which I did the worst thing I've ever done as a pastor.

I found a scapegoat.

The congregation knew I would be starting my forty day sabbatical as soon as the Sunday services were over. After preaching that morning and asking them to pray for me, I called the Worship Director into my office. I told him that after I came back I would be looking for a new Worship Director. I knew I was wrong as I was doing it – especially the timing. I even *told* him I knew I was wrong. Yet I did it anyway. I still don't know why. There were a lot of things wrong with the church at the time, including some issues in worship ministry of course, but there was far less wrong with him than there was with me.

Then I walked out of the church building and didn't talk to him or anyone else from the church for over five weeks.

I am still angry at myself for what I did to him that day. It has taken me far longer to forgive myself than it took him to forgive me. He led in worship for the next forty days without telling the congregation what I had done to him. The rest of the staff and volunteer leaders, led by Gary Garcia, my partner in ministry for over 20 years now, stepped up, served the people, prayed for me and wondered what would happen when the forty days were over.

For my part, I was determined that I wouldn't worry about the church, think about it or even drive past the building. And that's just what I did. Sometimes I had to devise interesting routes home in order to avoid it, which is *really* hard to do when you're trying not to think about it, but I succeeded. For forty days I never saw the property.

During that dark time I went to *The Center for Individual and Family Therapy* (CIFT) where Dr. Jim Masteller helped me figure out a lot of difficult things about myself.

The first thing we worked on was determining what exactly was wrong. For the first few sessions he just kept probing around, asking questions. He was trying to get me to admit to myself, not just what was wrong, but what I wanted. I can't remember exactly what led to this, but I remember very clearly blurting out to him in desperation, "I just need to fall in love with Jesus again!"

That became our goal. We quickly discovered that the only way I was going to get there was to get past my angry feelings that God had let me down. The first step in that process, Jim said, was to work on redefining success.

God hadn't let me down. I wasn't supposed to be someone else or somewhere else. God made me who I was and placed me where I was. I would never be OK with myself until I was OK with that.

Redefining success. The first time he brought up that idea, I bristled. I argued that redefining success was just a euphemism for settling for less. Yet he knew that's not what it was. Jim, a former pastor himself, recognized that my definition of success in ministry had become unbiblical and unhealthy. It was killing me from the inside-out, but God had protected me from reaching an unbiblical goal I had set for myself. My failure to reach that goal wasn't a problem, it was God's blessing.

Dr. Masteller didn't tell me what a new definition of success would look like. I'd have to figure that out for myself. This was truly a desert time for me, some of it literally, since I spent a week of it hiking in Joshua Tree National Park. By the time the forty days were over, I knew he was right. I wasn't healthy yet, but I was heading in the right direction and was equipped with the tools I needed to become healthy again.

A New Start

Three days before the first Sunday that I was due back in church, I received a call from one of the deacons. They were meeting that night and asked if I'd join them. I drove to the meeting nervously, not knowing what would happen.

We greeted each other with awkward but genuine smiles and hugs, then sat in the living room where one of them opened in prayer. They got right to the point. "Pastor," one of them said, "we wanted to talk with you tonight for two reasons. First, we want to know, is forty days enough? Or do you need more time? Because if you do, we'll figure out a way to make it work for you."

I was stunned. And grateful.

I should have asked them for another forty, but I didn't. I told them I was ready to be back on Sunday.

"Good," he said. "We were hoping you'd say that. The second reason we wanted to meet with you doesn't matter now. We were going to ask if you were coming back, or leaving for good. If you were planning to leave we were going to try to convince you to stay. Now all we have to do is welcome you home."

"Actually, there is one more issue we need to talk about," another deacon added. "You need to reconcile with (she mentioned the Worship Director by name) as soon as possible."

My heart was in my throat. They *knew*.

Then it hit me. They knew?! That meant they were fully aware of what I'd done and even though they made no effort to excuse it away, it hadn't stopped them from offering to help me or wanting me back as their pastor.

Grace is a beautiful thing.

That deacon offered to go with me to talk with the Worship Director if I wanted the emotional support. I accepted. My days of trying to do the hard stuff by myself were over. We met the following evening at the Worship Director's home. I repented of my actions and begged him and his wife for their forgiveness. They accepted my apology and forgave me completely although, given that they'd already started on plans for leaving, they did say goodbye to the church shortly thereafter. He and his wife remain our friends and we still enjoy each other's company when we see each other at birthdays and other celebrations.

To this day I stand in awe of how he did what he did, leading a hurting congregation in healing worship for the forty days I was gone without telling anyone outside the leadership what I'd done to him – and only then because they asked, as it turned out. It is a testimony to his character and another example of God's grace in action.

I'd like to say that things got better at the church right away, but they didn't. Many who had hung in to help through the crisis felt they could leave now, including many of the deacons who had been so gracious to me. Some left after word got out about what I'd done to the Worship Director, even though he begged them not to.

I understand why people left. I'd given them many reasons to leave and very few reasons to stay. They weren't leaving the church as much as they were leaving me. I'd have left me too.

To the people who stayed, prayed and worked through that brutal season and beyond it, I have just one thing to say, and it will never feel like enough.

Thank you.

Thinking Differently

Pastors talk a lot about how the church is a family. During those next two-plus rebuilding years, we became in action what we knew we were theologically.

Gradually I learned to stop worrying about how many people showed up for Sunday services. I was just glad they were there at all, and that they allowed me to be their pastor and their friend.

Soon I was having more good days than bad days, emotionally and spiritually. Eventually the bad days became rare. Soon the church started to regain its footing. Yes, the crowds were growing somewhat, but more than that, there was a sense of a fresh start. We weren't worried about where we were going next, but were content to enjoy the moments we had now. People were excited about the church and about inviting their friends again. I was healthy and so was the church.

Then, in early 2008, while meeting with the staff over ministry plans, I noticed some old habits trying to bore their way into my brain again. I was worrying about how to get more people in the seats and wondering which strategies we could employ from the latest pastoral help book I had read, when I stopped, looked at my staff and said, "we need to stop thinking like a big church."

I'll explain more about what that means in the following chapter, but for now let me say this. That was the day my perspective on church ministry changed for good, the day I discovered that I am a Small Church pastor, and the moment this book and the ministry of New Small Church was born.

Chapter 3
Stop Thinking Like a Big Church

The logic of the church growth movement went something like this:

- The mission of the church is to reach people for Jesus
- Reaching more people for Jesus is better than reaching fewer people for Jesus
- Churches that are reaching more people for Jesus will have more people in them and become big churches
- In order to become a big church you need to Think Like a Big Church

At the height of the church growth movement no phrase or concept was more repeated or firmly believed than that last one – Think Like a Big Church. I heard it everywhere. I told it to my church leaders too.

It was the main reason for some of the biggest mistakes of my ministry.

A Slight Diversion...

Before I go too far into this chapter, I want to add a postscript from the preceding chapter.

It's time to stop blaming Rick Warren.

I recently re-read *The Purpose Driven Church*, and seeing it with more mature eyes helped me understand that what happened to me after I first read it was not based on what he *wrote* in it, but on what I *read into* it. Rick never advocated that all churches should be huge, or that they would inevitably get there by following the principles in his book. He even opened the book by dedicating it to the hard-working Small Church bi-vocational pastors, whom he calls, "the true heroes of the faith." His point in the book was that all churches should discover what God's purpose is for them, then minister according to that purpose. And he's right.

That message gets twisted when the people who read his book and attend his Pastors' Schools, including me, go into it knowing about the growth and influence of Saddleback Church. We expect the book to give us the secret to duplicating that success. And we always find what we're looking for, even if it's not there, don't we?

When Rick illustrates how to apply Purpose Driven principles, he gives them from his own life and ministry, just as I do. The only reason the illustrations are megachurch illustrations is because he pastors a megachurch.

I've never met Rick Warren, and it's not like he needs my support or approval. I'm not even saying that I agree with him about everything – which you'll see in further chapters where his name comes up again. But I do think, for our own health and for the health of our churches, that pastors need to thank him for his gracious heart and stop blaming him for how we've misread the valuable message he has made available. Very few, if any, pastors have put their ideas and principles up for public use and public scrutiny as cheerfully and generously as he has.

Now where was I? Ah yes...

Stop thinking like a big church.

Should Every Pastor be a Rancher?

In the past several decades, the most common metaphor for explaining what it means to think like a big church is the shepherd/ rancher illustration. Under the shepherding model, the pastor takes care of the sheep one-on-one. Under the ranching model, the pastor trains a group of under-shepherds who do the day-to-day hands-on care, while the pastor's primary role shifts to overseeing the under-shepherds.

As the metaphor goes, sometimes, under the ranching model, we have to do spiritual triage. On a battlefield when the casualties are piling up, doctors at the start of triage may look uncaring as they walk past injured people and spend their time with healthy ones. But the healthy people they spend time with are nurses, medics and other doctors. They do this to train, share info and prioritize so they can serve more people with greater effectiveness.

In a big church, the ranching/spiritual triage model makes sense. There's no way one person can care for thousands of people individually. A well-trained team of staff and volunteers is essential to every aspect of ministry.

In a Small Church, when the pastor stops doing hospital visits, ceases having an open door policy and starts delegating those responsibilities to others, the congregation members feel neglected and unimportant.

Then they start looking for another church. I know. I've experienced it first-hand.

I'm not the only one with this experience. I've talked to many discouraged pastors with stories just like mine, who tried the rancher model only to find their congregation members feeling neglected.

That neglected feeling is understandable. After all, when Jesus commissioned Peter, he told him, "feed my sheep" not "tend my ranch". The ranching model tells us that our primary focus needs to move from "doing the caring" to "develop and manage a system of care" for the body we serve. There's just one problem with that. As a pastor friend of mine says, "People want to be pastored, not spiritually managed."

The rancher model doesn't automatically make pastors' lives easier or more productive, either. Many of us who tried the rancher model felt unfulfilled and ineffective because our heart was in hands-on ministry, but our schedules had shifted to leadership training, promotion and administration.

I wasn't called to manage systems. I was called to pastor people.

Very few pastors entered the ministry because they felt called to "develop and manage a system" of anything, let alone with the expectation that they would ever stop doing the caring themselves. And to be fair, promoters of the rancher system don't say the pastor should stop doing pastoral care, just that it needs to become a secondary priority, with the training of others taking precedence.

I agree that training and delegating others to do more aspects of ministry must be a higher priority in pastoral work than it often is. This lesson is as old as Moses – literally. The primary biblical argument for the rancher model comes from Jethro, Moses' father-in-law, who watched Moses work from dawn to dusk as the only judge for an entire nation of people. This was not serving God, Moses or the people well, so Jethro devised a plan of delegation that worked far better.

Ranching works. To argue that delegation and training are unnecessary is foolhardy, unbiblical and probably egotistical. After all, it was the Apostle Paul himself who told us that one of the primary jobs of pastors is, "to prepare God's people for works of service." Sounds like delegation to me.

But Jesus primarily used and taught the shepherding model, not the ranching model. For example, after his resurrection Jesus told Peter three times to "feed my sheep". In the first and third instances, the Greek word Jesus used for "feed" can literally be translated as "*pasture* my sheep." In the middle one, it means "*shepherd* my sheep." The English word *pastor* comes from those shepherding terms.

So it's true that both the ranching and shepherding models exist in scripture. But if we're going to be blunt about it, we have to admit that most of what we've picked up about ranching is not from scripture. It's from business and military practices. It's no coincidence that megachurches started proliferating on the heels of the post-WW2 rebuilding years. Megachurches simply adapted many of the top-down military efficiency methods that won the war and rebuilt nations.

There's nothing wrong with adapting outside methods, of course. Jethro was a priest of Midian, not of Israel, yet Moses learned from his wise counsel. And the fact that Jesus never directly referred to ranching doesn't mean we can't use it. But the balance of scripture unquestionably leans towards shepherding. That alone should make us pause a bit before we back-shelf the method Jesus made front and center.

Consider also that under the ranching model, Jesus' parable of the lost sheep would be very different. The rancher wouldn't have gone out to find the missing sheep himself, he would have trained and delegated under-shepherds to do that. What matters, of course, is that the lost sheep is found, not who does the finding – and ultimately only Jesus truly does the finding – but such stories should remind us that pastors who are called to serve predominantly in the shepherd role should not be made to feel like they have to justify that choice.

Jesus never stopped being a shepherd even though he often had huge crowds to take care of. Yes, he used the rancher model at times, like when he sent out the 70 to preach, then report back to him, and when he told the disciples to distribute the food to the 5,000-plus hungry people. But *shepherding* was always his primary mode of ministry.

Since Jesus constantly taught and used the shepherd model, but only occasionally taught or used the ranching model, shouldn't shepherding be our default setting too?

Even if you accept the premise that ranching is the best way to build and manage a big church, it may not be the best way to pastor a New Small Church. Yet take a look at the books and seminars espousing the ranching model. Do any of them admit that it may not be the best method for smaller congregations? None that I'm aware of.

Unquestionably, we should adopt the rancher model when it's needed. But I'm still looking for a pastoral ministry seminar or book teaching the ranching method that also cautions us to think long and hard before abandoning the shepherd model entirely.

Why is this rancher model so overwhelmingly dominant in our pastoral teaching? Because it's always assumed that anyone with vision is going to grow a big church. The sooner we adopt the rancher model, the sooner this inevitable growth will take place.

This ranching model was what I was walking away from when I told my church staff that we were going to stop thinking like a big church. That day we made a conscious decision to never again allow spiritual triage to be an excuse to manage systems at the expense of caring for people.

That doesn't mean we stopped training others to do the work of ministry — we redoubled our efforts at that. It did mean that we would never let the training of others become a reason for neglecting hands-on ministry ourselves.

In a megachurch, the pastor may indeed have to give up doing the caregiving in order to meet the needs and manage the necessary systems. In a Small Church the pastor can and should do both.

The True Price of the Megachurch

Big church systems work for big churches. But even when they do, it's important to let people know that, along with the great things that are gained when a church grows, even those gains carry a cost.

I was using a DVD series from a well-known megachurch pastor in the home group my wife and I host, when he said something that struck me as odd. As he stood in the lobby of his church he said, "Thousands of people walk through those doors every weekend, and sometimes I'll actually come out in the lobby and just watch the people as they come in … I love these people. These are some of the people I love more than anyone else on the earth."

Really? I thought. He loves the people of the church so much he *actually* goes to the lobby to *watch* them?

I don't doubt the love this pastor has for his church, and our home group gained a lot from his book and DVD series. But can you imagine anyone who loves someone "more than anyone else on earth" being content with just watching them? And stating that as proof of how much he loves them? Except a celebrity talking about their fans?

This pastor doesn't sit and talk with the members of his church when they come in for weekend services. He can't. There are too many of them. He has to settle for watching them instead.

It made me feel sad for him. I'm probably reading my own feelings into it, but I sensed he felt some sadness when he said it.

That's one of the prices megachurch pastors have to pay. I believe it is a significant price that costs them more than most people realize. I'm grateful to them for making that sacrifice because I don't know if I could remain emotionally and spiritually healthy if I were called upon to make the same sacrifice. Actually, my history is proof that I couldn't.

We need megachurches. We really do. But we need to follow the advice of Jesus before we just keep building bigger and bigger ones. We need to count the cost. And the cost is more than monetary – far more. The real cost is the human one. And no one pays that price more than the megachurch pastors themselves – except maybe their spouses and kids. As megachurch pastor Mark Driscoll recently tweeted, "Your pastor may be the loneliest guy in your church and unless you are him that probably doesn't make much sense at all." That feeling isn't exclusive to megachurch pastors, but I think it's noteworthy that it was a megachurch pastor who felt the need to tweet it.

Before Rob Bell became a lightning rod for his teachings on the existence/non-existence of hell, he was a pastor who wrote about the emotional and spiritual cost of such rapid church growth, and what he called "Church incorporated" in his break-through book *Velvet Elvis.* He described the panic that led him to hide in the storage room of the church on a Sunday morning, debating driving away from it all. The problem? His young church had experienced unprecedented, immediate growth, and he wasn't prepared to handle it.

When I first read Bell's account, while I was disarmed by his honesty, my first response wasn't very sympathetic. It was more like *sorry Rob, I'm having a hard time relating to the trauma of too much success too fast. Get back to me when you've had years of pounding your head against a brick wall trying to get people to show up, or losing a lot of the people you've already got. That's something I can relate to.*

That part of Bell's story seemed whining and diva-esque to me at the time. It doesn't seem that way now. One of the primary lessons of church history is that it's harder to serve Christ in times of success than failure.

It's been said that if you want to last long-term in ministry, stay away from the three Gs – the Girls, the Gold and the Glory. Yes, that's a bit dated and sexist, but that's what the saying was.

There's a lot of Glory coming your way when thousands of people show up every week to sit silently and listen carefully to every word you have to say. Not everyone can handle it. Some melt down temporarily like Rob Bell described, others permanently. Some let it go to their heads and start thinking they deserve all the accolades. Still others feel that since they've been able to handle the Glory so well, they deserve to go after the Girls and the Gold too. Church history is littered with the scandals and collateral damage caused by such twisted thinking.

It's one of the reasons I have such a high admiration for megachurch pastors who are able to maintain their composure and humility to keep healthy megachurches growing and going for decades.

Pastoring a healthy megachurch is a special and rare gift. I have learned to be grateful that I have not been burdened with it.

Small, Big, Mega… Is there a Venti?

Before we go any further, let's define some terms. Sounds exciting right? Hang in there. This stuff actually matters. I'll make it as pain-free as possible, I promise.

When we make distinctions between small , big, or megachurch, what do we mean, exactly?

Numerically, the boundaries between churches of each size are fairly fluid, but here's what I mean by the following:
- House Church: Less than 25 (and meeting in a house)
- Small Church: 25 – 350 (or under 25 meeting in a church building)
- Big Church: 350 – 2,000
- Megachurch: Over 2,000

Within some categories, church size distinctions could be broken down even further. For instance, there are clearly two distinct levels of Small Churches. A typical Small Church is 25 – 200, while churches from 200 – 350 might be called midsize.

But, as with everything in the church, numbers aren't always the best way to make these distinctions. At various size levels, churches actually take on a new personality. This shift means that churches of 200 – 350 in weekend attendance, while still considered small, have a personality and management type that is very different from those at 25 – 200.

These shifts in church personality may actually be a more accurate way of defining each size.

- House Church – Run as a single family unit. Everyone participates in everything.

- Small Church – Strong pastoral control. Ministries are mostly offered by age categories.

- Midsize Church –Some staff is hired and ministries are available based on interests and needs.

- Big Church – More program-oriented. Pastoral ministry is done by staff pastors and in small groups. A very high quality is expected in all programs and ministries.

- Megachurch – Operates much like a group of Small Churches meeting niche needs. They gather under a common name and Lead Pastor for weekend services. Most attenders do not see the Lead Pastor outside of the preaching time. The Lead Pastor is a leader of leaders, pastoring the church staff.

A Small Church has less than 350 in average weekend attendance. But when I use the term Small Church I don't include house churches for a couple of reasons.

First, house churches are a unique sector of church life that operate on significantly different principles than other churches. While I appreciate them and am grateful for the people they serve, especially in parts of the world where the church has been driven underground, I have zero experience or expertise in them and wouldn't presume to teach about them.

Second, just as there is plenty of information about how to run a megachurch, there are also plenty of books and websites about house churches. My goal is to tackle the middle ground between the house church and the megachurch where the vast majority of churches are, but where there has been very little support, encouragement or teaching.

Chapter 4

Don't Despise the Size

All the people we saw there are of great size. ... We seemed like grasshoppers in our own eyes, and we looked the same to them.
— Numbers 13:32-33

Don't let anyone look down on (despise – KJV) you because you are young. — 1 Timothy 4:12

Size matters not. Look at me. Judge me by size, do you? – Yoda

I spent too many years telling good people that the way they wanted to do church was wrong.

These people weren't heel-draggers or vision-killers. Not all of them. Not most of them.

They weren't the grasshoppers. I was.

They were followers of Jesus who attended the church I was pastoring because they found their spiritual and emotional needs met there. And they felt inspired enough by the spiritual guidance they received to want to share it with others.

They didn't need me or anyone else telling them they weren't doing it right simply because one of the main things that attracted them to the church – its small, personal nature – was somehow inadequate, or worse, a mistake. But I did tell them that. Through myriad subtle and not-so-subtle teachings and behaviors, I did to them what had been done to me. I made them feel less valued because they weren't as big as some false sense of success told them they should be.

If Big Equals Successful, What Does Small Equal?

Big things can be inspiring.

They can also be intimidating.

When the Hebrew spies checked out the Promised Land, they all came back with the same report. *It's a great land! A wealthy land! A HUGE land!* Two of them were inspired by the massive size of it, the other ten were intimidated.

When Paul appointed Timothy to pastor the fledgling Ephesian church, Timothy was so young that Paul felt it necessary to remind Timothy not to let anyone despise his young age.

I hate to admit this, but as a Small Church pastor I have allowed myself to feel intimidated and despised by big church pastors on many occasions.

Most Small Church pastors know the feeling. We have a culture, especially in the western, anglo church, of equating size with success. Thus, every book I have ever read about various church sizes begins with the premise that churches of one size need to remove whatever obstacles are stopping them from becoming a church of the next size larger. Onward and upward.

Here are the American stats, according to Carl F. George: "At the 100 mark, your church has become larger than 60 percent of your peers'; at 140, 75 percent; at 200, 80 percent; at 350, 93 percent; and by 500, 95 percent."

So 93% of American churches (under 350) are small, while 80% (under 200) are very small. If size equals success, then 93% of pastors are unsuccessful, bad at their jobs and inadequate at fulfilling their calling, while 80% are *very* bad at their jobs – a number I escape being a part of, but *barely.*

So 80% to 93% of pastors are failures? Can that be right?

No. Half of all Christians in America, and far more than half of Christians worldwide attend a Small Church, not because they lack options, but – shockingly – they go to a Small Church *because they want to!* And no one has the right to tell them they are wrong to feel that way. Wanting to worship and serve God in a Small Church is not a theological error or a personality deficit. It's time we stopped treating it as though it was.

We'll get into some of the reasons why most people choose Small Churches over big churches in the coming chapters. But for now, Small Church pastors, take note of this. The next time you're tempted to get frustrated about how many people are driving past your church to attend a megachurch, realize that there are more people who drive past megachurches to attend a Small Church.

Before we can get to more of that good news, we need to take a hard look at how Small Churches and those who pastor them are perceived by some people. As I said before, my feelings of inadequacy at being a Small Church pastor were my own doing. But they weren't formed in a vacuum.

Unfortunately, most pastors take our cues about how we feel towards our Small Church, not from the people who attend and love it, but from attitudes like those expressed in the following true stories.

Is There Anything Wrong With a Church Being Small?

Years ago, I attended a pastoral conference where the keynote speaker was the pastor of a megachurch. After two days of often helpful and inspiring advice about how to overcome church growth barriers, mostly taken from anecdotes about the spectacular growth of his church, he took questions from the audience.

One of the first questions was from the pastor of a small, struggling church. "I've heard a lot of good things in the last couple days about overcoming obstacles and bringing numerical growth to the church," he said. "And I've been trying to apply these principles in my church for years now. What I was wondering was, is there anything wrong with a church being small?"

"No," answered the megachurch pastor, "not for two weeks."

The Small Church pastor chuckled uncomfortably, then waited for a smile, a "just kidding" or some further explanation from the megachurch pastor. It never came. The Small Church pastor turned and walked away. Another person came to the mic with another question. The conference went on.

Just a year or so after that exchange, I was at a conference where they had a debate about ministers and tithing. Some felt that a minister's tithe belonged entirely to their home church. Others made the case that it would be OK for a minister to pay some or all their tithe to a denomination. This was based on the premise that a minister's denomination is their spiritual authority, much like church leaders are for church members.

One bi-vocational pastor argued that the tithe on his income from ministry pay could properly go to a denomination, but he believed that any tithe made from secular employment belongs to the local church alone. As one way of making his case, he told the assembled ministers that his small, struggling, low-income church could not survive without his tithe from secular work.

"If your church is too small to survive without your tithe," a minister on the other side of the argument answered, "maybe it shouldn't survive at all."

I later heard that the minister who made that statement went to the bi-vocational pastor after the meeting to offer an apology. But as far as I know, that statement was never retracted in public.

Those two examples may be extreme, but they are real. And they are telling. With attitudes like that in play, how can Small Church pastors not feel despised?

Who's Despising Who?

I have actually paused at my laptop keyboard for quite a while, struggling whether-or-not to type this next paragraph because I don't want it to be true. Perhaps it's just my inner grasshopper speaking, but here goes...

For the last several decades, the church leadership culture as a whole has despised Small Churches.

Very few church leaders would say something as despicable as you heard in the previous stories, but we give out the same message, mostly unintentionally, in so many other ways.

For instance, it's possible that this may be the first time you've heard anyone espouse the idea that Small Churches are not just OK, but are to be celebrated as essential members of the body of Christ. I know that for one simple reason. As I mentioned on the preface page, after looking for years to find a book that would encourage me in my role as a Small Church pastor, I finally gave up looking and decided to write it myself.

There's something wrong with that, isn't there?

Unfortunately, the despising isn't a one-way street. You don't have to spend long in the company of Small Church pastors to hear the bile flow the other way. Just bring up the name of the latest local big church success story and the pettiness will begin. "They water down the Gospel," "The pastor is beholden to a handful of wealthy donors," "He's only there because he's related to so-and-so," "They're just stealing sheep from other churches," etc.

For many of us, those feelings are the elephant in the room that I'm not supposed to point out. But if that's what I'm doing I'm in good company. Jesus did it all the time. Have we forgotten what happened when Jesus' disciples were despising each other?

> When he (Jesus) was in the house, he asked them, "What were you arguing about on the road?" But they kept quiet because on the way **they had argued about who was the greatest**. Sitting down, Jesus called the Twelve and said, "If anyone wants to be first, he must be the very last, and the servant of all." (Mark 9:33-35) (emphasis mine)

Arguing about who's the greatest. There is truly nothing new under the sun. Even our petty arguments are recycled.

So who's the greatest? Megachurches with their beautiful facilities, media ministries and excellent programs for meeting any imaginable need? Or Small Churches with their personal touch and tight-knit relationships?

Are there some churches that are too small to be worthy of their existence? Or is it possible that churches of each size have their own blessings to bring, their own niche to fill and their own responsibility to God for using the gifts they've been given?

A Great Church, or a Great *Little* Church?

I've come to realize a valuable truth in recent years. I'm a really good pastor. And I serve a really good church – not just a good *little* church.

It's interesting, isn't it, that when people compliment the ministries of a big church they say "it's a great church". But when they compliment a Small Church they always say something like "it's a great *little* church." Or, even worse, "it's a wonderful church, *for its size.*"

It's like telling someone "you look good *for your age,*" isn't it? Doesn't that extra kicker just give you the warm fuzzies?

The truth is there are great churches that are big and great churches that are small.

I pastor a great church. No further adjectives are needed.

To My Friends Who Pastor Small Churches

Most Small Churches are struggling.

We struggle to pay the bills, we struggle to recruit volunteers, we struggle with inadequate or non-existent facilities, we struggle to open the front door wider and close the back door tighter. Most of these struggles are unavoidable. They're just the cost of doing Small Church.

There's one struggle we can lay aside if we choose to, though. The struggle to be something we aren't.

We no longer need to live up to someone else's expectations or, worse, to our own unreasonable, unbiblical expectations.

Yes, fellow would-be grasshoppers, there are giants in the land. Giant churches with giant budgets, casting giant shadows. But these giants are not our enemies. To use another biblical example, they are not Goliath to our David.

Instead, we need to use one more biblical analogy. Perhaps big churches are the bicep, while Small Churches are the little toe in the body of Christ. It's about cooperation, not competition. We need to learn to be who God made us to be, taking orders from our common head. Let's get some communication and cooperation going between the little toe and the bicep. Then maybe this body that's bigger than all of us can actually start doing the "greater things" Jesus promised we would do.

Jealousy is no way to build a great church of any size. Neither is fear, doubt or self-loathing.

In Paul's body illustration in 1 Corinthians 12, he notes that the despising within the body happens in two distinct ways. The verses we usually quote are "The eye cannot say to the hand, 'I don't need you!' and the head cannot say to the feet, "I don't need you!'" But Paul actually begins the body analogy, not by addressing the parts that despise other parts, but by speaking to the parts that despise themselves.

"If the foot should say, 'Because I am not a hand, I do not belong to the body,' it would not for that reason cease to be part of the body."

Self-despising is where Paul begins the metaphor because self-despising is where all despising begins.

If we won't despise our (small) size, we'll have no reason to despise their (large) size.

To My Friends Who Pastor Big Churches

We are on the same team.

I'm grateful when you are there to help me and other Small Church pastors. But I also want you to know that we are here to help you too.

There is a lot we can learn from each other.

It's important for me to say that I have met very few big church pastors who harbor the attitude expressed by the pastors I described earlier in this chapter. When megachurch pastors hold conferences, I know they do it to provide a service to fellow ministers, and many offer discounts, scholarships and outright free tuition for many pastors who couldn't otherwise afford it.

So I don't question anyone's motives. But I do question some presumptions, because we all share them.

Even now, many of you are having an internal argument with my premise that a lot of churches are called by God to be Small Churches. I will never convince many pastors, from churches of all sizes, that small is ever OK because being OK with being small feels like giving in to mediocrity. I know the feeling. One book wouldn't have been enough to convince me of it either.

For those who find yourself arguing that no church should be OK with being small, consider this. We all know that a big church should have small group ministries. After all, churches should grow big and grow small at the same time. If so, why are small groups important?

I would propose that small groups are needed in big churches for the same reasons Small Churches are needed in the body of Christ. Because they offer unique opportunities for fellowship, ministry, commitment, worship and discipleship that you can't get if you're only a part of a larger group.

No pastor despises the role of home group leaders in their church so, if it helps, let's look at Small Church pastors as the home group leaders of the body of Christ.

No one needs to feel bad for Small Church pastors because our church is small any more than you'd feel bad for your small group leaders because their groups are small. Being small is a big part of why those groups exist and why they work. The same goes for Small Churches. Being small is a major part of why so many of us exist and why our ministries work. Many of us find great fulfillment in ministry because we know we fill a role in the kingdom of God that only we can fill.

I do believe that we need to celebrate ministries who experience numerical growth, especially if that growth isn't transfer growth. But while we celebrate those stories, we need to figure out a way to celebrate the less visible successes of churches whose weekend worship attendance numbers don't seem to change much from year to year.

To all my friends who pastor large and/or growing churches, I want to let you off the hook. The next time we talk about how our ministries are going, there's no need to change the subject, cheer me up or look away awkwardly when I tell you our weekend worship attendance hasn't grown again this year. I don't feel bad about it, and neither should you.

The fact that my church is small doesn't mean I've failed to fulfill my potential. I am where I want to be, and I'm pretty sure it's where God wants me, too.

I'm happy for you and your church, and I hope you can be happy for me and mine – I certainly am.

If It Ain't Broke...

A friend of mine, who has spent decades of ministry in Latin America, has had a front-row seat to one of the world's greatest revivals. Throughout Latin America people are coming to a saving knowledge of Jesus, being healed of diseases and transforming their communities from the inside-out. Almost entirely in Small Churches.

Church growth experts have been travelling there for years to study this phenomenal revival and some have reported their findings to my friend. Their conclusions? The revival is legitimate, it is theologically sound and it is culturally organic. There's just one problem, according to these experts. The churches are too small. So the experts have proposed to my friend that further study needs to be done in order to "fix" this "problem".

Sure, we could "fix" the problem of Small Churches popping up daily throughout Latin America. The result would be the same as when my vet "fixed" my dog. We'd tame it, make it less aggressive, more passive and guarantee that it would never reproduce again.

Small ≠ broken.

We Can Do Better

OK, fellow Small Church pastors, now that all this "everybody's so mean to me" whining is done, what are we going to do about it?

Let's start by acknowledging what we all know. Very few of us are coming close to doing the task we're called to do and are capable of. Yes, there is far more good ministry being done in Small Churches than we're usually made aware of, but the flip-side of that is also true.

A lot of Small Churches are not very good, and that's why they're small.

We are grasshoppers by choice.

We can do better. Much better. We have to.

How to do that is what the last two-thirds of this book is about.

Chapter 5

Why We Need Churches of All Sizes

Every size of church has value.

The Grasshopper Myth isn't the result of *being* small. It comes from *feeling* small and believing those feelings.

New Small Churches have discovered who they are and how to utilize their unique gifts. That includes the advantages that come, not in spite of their size, but *because* of their size.

IKEA Envy

IKEA and Starbucks.

Virtually no one had heard of those two companies 20 years ago. Today they each dominate their sector of the marketplace and have become iconic international brands.

They have nothing in common. Except their success.

One sells assemble-it-yourself furniture in massive stores (some so big you have to wonder if they're visible from space) with arrows on the floor to push you through a maze of options. They make people feel happy because their furniture costs far less money than people used to have to pay.

The other sells made-to-order coffee in *small* stores (some so small they fit neatly tucked inside the corners of other stores), with a relaxed hang-out-wherever-you-want atmosphere. They make people feel happy paying *more* money than they used to pay for a cup of coffee.

No one in their right mind would look at either business model and call it a failure.

If the corporate world approached success and growth the way many church leaders do, you might be able to imagine the executives from Starbucks getting together for their annual planning meeting to hear the following report from their Store Growth Task Force:

Currently, the average Starbucks store is less than 800 square feet. We have sent out our spies with measuring tapes and they have discovered that the average IKEA store is well over 100,000 square feet. Some are as large as 200,000 square feet! And our current trend of placing Starbucks locations inside other businesses like grocery stores, entertainment venues and banks is lowering the average store size even more.

In the opinion of this Task Force, this is simply unacceptable. If we hope to compete with IKEA, we need to increase the size of the average Starbucks location, and we need to get started NOW!

In the brochures we've handed out, you will find a multi-year strategy that, in the opinion of this Task Force, we must implement immediately:
  - *Hold grow-your-store seminars, starting immediately. Shamefully, most of our franchisees know little or nothing about how to build a bigger store, and most of them are*

content to just keep serving coffee in the same small store location

- *Launch a Bigger Stores Make Better Coffee campaign to motivate store growth and encourage the acquisition and launching of new Large Store properties*
- *Require all Starbucks stores that currently rent space inside another retail outlet to purchase their own property for a larger stand-alone Starbucks, following our five-year timeline*
- *Drop franchisees whose stores don't meet a minimum limit of square footage and combine their assets with nearby stores to buy land and build larger stores*
- *Change the name Starbucks to STARBUCKS*

Hey! Get Yer Own Mission!

So what's my point in this mini-parable? That Small Churches shouldn't try to grow? Obviously not.

My point is that each church has its own mission and shouldn't try to duplicate the mission of another church, no matter how successful or large that other church is.

Starbucks is great at being Starbucks. IKEA is great at being IKEA.

They're so different that they're not even in competition with each other. Neither are megachurches and Small Churches.

Starbucks trying to be IKEA is unnecessary. Starbucks trying to be IKEA while still being Starbucks (or STARBUCKS) is a joke.

Some churches offer one product and brew it well. Others offer multiple products for varying tastes. Some churches offer personalized choices allowing everyone to explore Biblical truths at their own pace. Others are highly structured IKEA-type "arrows on the floor" experiences that offer a more orderly approach.

What's the best approach?

All of them.

And none of them.

Each type has something for someone, while even the *best* churches turn some people off. Many people who love the way Starbucks approaches their business *can't stand* the way IKEA does it – and vice versa. Still other people are repelled by the corporate nature of both of them, preferring to support local neighborhood stores with no corporate backing.

People approach church in the same way.

Just as Starbucks and IKEA have different types of businesses, different churches have different missions. Starbucks stores are small, not because they are failing, but because that's what works for them, their product, their current customers and the customers they are still trying to win over.

What works for one may not work for another. No one style works everywhere. No one size fits all.

Our Problem May Not Be a Problem

As we saw earlier, 93% of American churches are smaller than 350, and 85% are smaller than 200. What if those percentages aren't a problem? What if that's the way it's supposed to be?

What if, when Jesus said, "I will build my church," he didn't see a world filled just with megachurches and grand cathedrals? What if he saw a world with a few megachurches and cathedrals, a larger number of mid-sized-to-big churches and hundreds of thousands of small way-stations of faith scattered around the globe, tucked into every community?

According to Reggie McNeal, "one-half of churchgoers attended churches in the top 10 percent of church size." That means the other half attended churches in the low 90% of church size, under 350 people. In any other service industry, if half the people were drawn to a specific way of receiving what they had to offer, they'd find ways to serve those people according to their chosen needs instead of trying to convince people that the way they want it is wrong.

As pastors, we're constantly telling people to be satisfied with how God made them. To know their gifts and discover their purpose. That there's a place for everyone in the body of Christ, no matter what you can or can't do. Maybe it's time to take a dose of our own advice, pastors and church leaders, and find out what's *right* about the current ratio of Small Churches to big churches.

A recent American Express TV commercial stated, "Entrepreneurs are the most powerful force in the economy – the reinvention of business begins with them." No one disagrees with that. Small business is the engine that drives every economy. I believe the same can be said for Small Churches in relationship to the church as a whole. Could it be that Small Churches, if they are turned loose to be what they were meant to be, can have the same impact on the world for the sake of the Gospel?

Maybe, instead of Small Churches taking their lead from big churches, New Small Churches ought to get healthy and vibrant and start doing some leading of their own.

Why Many People Like Small to Mid-Sized Churches

Many people like an IKEA-sized church. Most like a Starbucks-sized one.

When I go on vacation I lean towards the IKEA-type churches – for the same reasons I like staying at a name-brand hotel instead of Joe's Motel, Bar & Grill. I don't need opulence (I'm a Small Church pastor – I can't *afford* opulence) but I want a minimal level of excellence and cleanliness with no surprises.

Since I don't get many weekends off, when I visit a church on vacation I like having some assurance that my church experience will meet a basic level of quality too. I know I'll get that in a megachurch because you can't get to mega size without some serious quality control. Sure, I'll miss out on some surprises and some homegrown charm that way, but I'm willing to give up some of the local character for consistency.

I get enough surprises when I'm vacationing somewhere I've never been. In church and in my hotel I want familiarity, quality and comfort. I want to be served. I want the staff to smile, act as if it's the greatest joy in their life to serve me and cater to my every whim. But I don't expect them to have a passing thought about me after I walk out the door.

When I come home I don't want to live in a hotel – not even a nice one. Some people do, but most people are like me. I don't want to feel like a guest being served in my own home, or my home church. I want to live in a smaller, less perfect home than the Hilton.

When I'm at home I don't need or want my sheets changed every day and turned down every evening with a mint on the pillow. In the same way, I don't want an overly programmed mood pre-set when I come to church. Don't try to control how I feel or, even worse, tell me what I *should* feel. Let me feel how I feel, and let me, my interactions with others and the Holy Spirit set the tone and the mood.

I want to feel intimate and cozy in my home and my home church. I want to be a participant in the process, not a customer. I'm willing to live with a little clutter and a bit of inconsistency if that's what it takes to feel at home, needed, wanted and missed when I'm not around.

People Have a Greater Personal Stake in What Happens

According to a recent study, "Those who attend megachurches are likelier to volunteer less, contribute less financially..." than their Small Church counterparts. The study cites evidence that 45% of megachurch attendees never volunteer their time at the church, 32% give nothing or very little in the offering, 40% don't belong to a small group, and 42% admitted they have very few close friends at the church.

In other words, megachurches are just like the rest of us. They have problems too.

It makes sense that Small Churches on the whole have more problems with issues like quality control and meeting budgets. It also makes sense that one of the reasons people go to megachurches is that they can disappear into the crowd. They can be observers instead of participants. That's not as easy to do in a Small Church.

One of the reasons people go to Small Churches is that its smaller size allows them to have a more personal stake in what happens. They know they matter.

The desire to feel needed is an essential human instinct. Megachurches can offer the overworked single mom or the high-pressure 70-hour-a-week executive a chance to finally *not* feel the demands of being needed for an hour or so on Sunday morning. Small Churches give people who spend their week in a dead-end job or alone in the house, the knowledge that someone cares, that what they do matters and that they're missed when they're not around.

The kingdom of Heaven is built on such as these.

Chapter 6

So What's Wrong with Church Growth?

What's wrong with church growth?

In a word, nothing.

But there are some significant problems with the church growth *strategies* we've been using for the past generation or so.

I'm not the only one who thinks so. The research is in.

In *The Present Future,* Reggie McNeal offers a scathing indictment of the church growth movement and its obsession with numbers. He believes, as I do, that while there were some good things to come out of the church growth movement, there was a lot of damage caused by it as well. Despite the desire of church growth advocates for their strategies to reach the unchurched, that doesn't seem to be how it's played out. Reflecting on some very reliable statistical analysis, McNeal concludes that, "with rare exception the 'growth' here was the cannibalization of the smaller membership churches by these emerging superchurches."

In addition, I'm not alone in having felt belittled by the church growth movement's obsession with numbers. It, and the corresponding "rise of the celebrity-status church culture," according to McNeal, "has created thousands of 'losers,' pastors and church leaders who are not serving in high-profile, high-growth churches. Consequently, a large part of the leadership of the North American church suffers from debilitation and even depression fostered by a lack of significance. The army of God has a lot of demoralized leaders."

The grasshoppers are multiplying.

From my perspective, there are four problems that have plagued us in our obsession with numerical growth in the church.

Problem #1: It is Growth-Oriented, Not Health-Oriented

Even though almost every church growth strategy claims that health is their goal, the assumption always follows that once you're healthy, you'll grow numerically.

The testimonies usually go something like this: "My church struggled for years trying to grow, then I went to this conference and/or read that book and decided not to worry about growth any more. I was just going to apply the principles I learned, bathe it in prayer and let God take care of the rest. As soon as I stopped *worrying* about growing, we *started* growing. Now let me show you the plans for our new mini-mall megaplex worship center."

I have no doubt that this has happened. And I am truly grateful to God for lives that have been changed because of growing, healthy churches. But the end result of these testimonies is still numerical growth. The health of the church is not seen as the end result, but as a means to an end. That's a problem. Health should be the goal.

As an alternative let me take the same testimony, change a few components and tell you my experience.

"My church struggled for years trying to grow. I went to conferences and read books, but my church didn't grow no matter how hard I worked and prayed. Out of sheer frustration I decided I wasn't going to worry about growth any more. I was just going to preach the word, feed the flock, minister to the community and let God take care of the rest. As soon as I stopped worrying about growing, my church and I started getting healthy again. It's been almost five years now, and we still haven't had any dramatic numerical growth, and I don't ever expect to, because a big part of being healthy is that we realized who we are. We're a Small Church and I am a Small Church pastor. Now let me tell you about some of the health*ful* ministry we've done that could never have been accomplished if we'd kept focusing our energies on becoming a big church."

Health has become our goal. For us and for those we minister to. Weekend worship, butts-in-the-seats numerical growth may never happen. We're OK with that.

Problem #2: It is Problem-Oriented

One of the better conferences and books I have attended and read was Christian Schwarz's *Natural Church Development* strategy. What made his principles different from the strategies that preceded it was that he really tried to solve Problem #1 and be more health-oriented than growth-oriented. As he pointed out in the conference, the title of his book and the strategy behind it is *Natural Church **Development***, not *Natural Church **Growth***.

What *wasn't* different in his strategy was that, like all the others, it is problem-oriented. The focus, as usual, was to *find the cause of the problem and fix it*. While the causes were different for each church, the problem was always the same – your church is too small.

The problem with a problem orientation (and no, the irony of describing the problems with a problem-orientation in a section where I'm listing four problems isn't lost on me) is that it assumes being small is a problem without considering any of the positive aspects of being small.

Instead of being *problem*-oriented, we need to be – no, don't read it before I write it, I'm not going there. Being *solutions*-oriented isn't any better, because you don't need to find a solution to something that isn't a problem to begin with. A solutions orientation still presumes that being small is a problem – and that *presumption* is a problem!

Instead of looking at Small Churches as places filled with problems that need to be solved, with walls that need to be climbed, barriers that need to be broken or ministries that need to be mended, maybe we should start looking at some of the advantages of being small.

Many pastoral help books have quoted the wonderful parable in the book *Soar With Your Strengths* about the school for animals. In this school, a little rabbit excelled in the running and jumping classes, but failed the flying and swimming tests. He was told that he needed to work on his weak areas, so he was taken out of the running class and doubled up on swimming lessons. As a result, the little rabbit was miserable. He never got any better at swimming and he started hating school altogether. The lesson of the parable and of the book is ducks gotta swim, eagles gotta soar and rabbits gotta run. We all need to do what we're good at without stressing over the things we're not.

Now let me get back to the thought I interrupted in mid-sentence three paragraphs back.

Instead of being *problem*-oriented, we need to be (here it comes) ~~strengths~~-oriented. We need to apply the *Soar With Your Strengths* principles to Small Churches. Stop worrying about what Small Churches are *not* good at and start appreciating and promoting what we *are* good at.

Positive reinforcement is a powerful tool. And I'm not talking about the Stuart Smalley, "I'm good enough, I'm smart enough and doggone it, people like me" school of pretending-I'm-great-without-having-anything-to-back-it-up. I mean, let's find out what some of the advantages of Small Churches really are. Those strengths do exist. I've seen them in action. We'll talk about some of them in the *Only in a Small Church* chapter, but for now we have another problem with the church growth movement to address (again, the irony).

Problem #3: It is Too Narrowly Focused

"Jesus wants the church to grow!"

I agree. How can I not? Jesus was the one who said, "I will build my church," and I've found that arguing with him is not a recipe for health or happiness.

"Jesus wants *your* church to grow!"

Wait just a second.

We often make that second statement as though it's the same thing as the first. It's not.

The church growth movement tends to be focused on the growth of individual congregations. Sometimes that's expanded, usually through a denominational strategy, to include a multiple-church plan, including church planting, but a denominational focus is too narrow also.

What if, as I said earlier, when Jesus said, "I will build my church," what he had in mind wasn't a world filled with grand cathedrals and megachurches? What if the current breakdown of 90% Small Churches to 10% medium-, big- and megachurches, instead of being a problem to solve, is actually closer to what Jesus intended?

If that's even a possibility, shouldn't we look into the idea of taking Small Churches more seriously?

Maybe getting Small Churches to become big churches isn't the answer to the problems that are stifling the growth of the western church in recent decades. After all, in the places where the church is growing the fastest, like in Latin America and Africa, New Small Churches are popping up all over the place. Sure, they have megachurches too, but megachurches aren't what's fueling some of the greatest revivals the world has ever seen. It's mostly happening in New Small Churches.

Maybe what Jesus had in mind was a world littered with churches of all sizes, shapes and styles to meet needs of all sizes, shapes and styles.

When my vision is limited to growing *my* church, instead of participating in what Jesus is doing to build *his* church, there's a tendency to invest our precious resources, both human and material, in the wrong places. If my church is supposed to be one of the small, wiry, guerrilla-style outposts, I'm not being a good steward of its resources when I pump my time, energy and money into trying to be a megachurch.

So that begs the question – if Small Churches can be so great, why does it seem like there are so many Small Churches, but so few *great* Small Churches?

First of all, that is only true in the western developed world, not in the developing world. But in the places where it *is* true, one of the reasons has to be our decades-long insistence on numerical growth as a measure (or *the* measure) of success. How is the pastor of a Small Church supposed to build a great church if they don't know their church can be both great *and* small?

Problem #4: Size Matters – But Not the Way We Think It Does

According to Lyle Schaller, "Churches have more in common by size than by their denomination, tradition, location, age, or any other single isolatable factor." If that's true, and I believe it is, we need to start thinking along those lines about the growth of the Church around the world.

What characteristics are shared by churches within a specific size-range? And what makes those churches ideally suited to certain roles in the body of Christ? I'm not suggesting some form of centralized organizational structure – Paul was very clear in his body analogy that we have one head, many parts. And that head is Christ, not a centralized bureaucracy. But the parts need to start thinking more holistically. One critical step towards that holistic thinking is to start seeing the advantages of varying sizes and styles of congregations.

Let's stop arguing about which size is best, and start seeing what's best about each size.

Specifically, what do Small Churches have in common? And what about their nature and structure makes them ideally suited for their unique place in the body of Christ?

In other words, what can Small Churches do that big churches can't do?

Chapter 7

Only In a Small Church

There are a lot of things big churches can do that Small Churches can't do. Large group meetings, regional evangelism crusades, big-name concerts, conferences and city-wide gatherings for instance. Big churches also have the space and administrative muscle to run K-12 schools, colleges and universities. Big churches can assemble massive resources when a large-scale deployment of people and money is needed to respond to disasters. Every week they have the capacity to offer multiple options for worshippers that Small Churches can't come close to duplicating.

There are also some great things Small Churches can do that big churches can't.

As an example, not long ago I had a conversation that reminded me why I pastor a Small Church. I had just finished the Sunday morning services when a young man in his mid-twenties approached me with a concerned look on his face.

He asked if we could talk and I said I'd be happy to. So after shaking a few hands as people left the building, I led him to my office where he told me this was the first time he'd ever been in this church.

He had been raised in a different part of the state, but recently he'd moved to go to university and had stopped attending church as he started partying with some new friends. For the past year or so he'd been following the lead of these new friends and was bedding every girl he could find – and he'd found a lot. For the past several weeks he'd been on a break from school and was staying in a town near our church where he was on a work-study project. At night he was chatting with girls online, then meeting them for sex.

"Last night," he told me, "I got together with a girl I'd met online. When we got going heavy into it I found out..." he looked at me with fright and shame, "I found out it wasn't a girl." Tears started down his cheeks. "Pastor, how did I let this happen? How did I put myself in a position where someone could deceive me like that? I'm a Christian. Why am I doing this?"

I let him get it all out. The guilt, the anger, the hurt. For about five minutes he poured his heart out to me, a man he'd never met, until he was empty. He ended with this question: "Pastor, how did I get so weak?"

"You're not weak" I told him. "What you just did in the last ten minutes is one of the gutsiest things I've ever seen. You walked into a strange church, approached the pastor, then confessed the greatest sins of your life to him. You had no idea what my response would be. You didn't know if I'd be disgusted or sympathetic, if I'd be angry or merciful. If you have enough strength to do that, you have enough strength to resist any temptation that comes your way. You just need to repent of this behavior, re-commit your life to following Christ, then use the courage you've displayed today to do what you know is right, despite what your newfound friends want you to do. Oh, and get some new friends."

I walked him through a prayer of repentance, assured him of God's forgiveness and helped encourage him to be the man of God we both knew he could be.

Before he left I asked him why he had come to our church. We live in Orange County California, so we're not exactly hurting for church options for him.

"I looked you up on the internet" he told me. "I wanted a small church because I knew that was the only place where I would be able to meet with the pastor on a Sunday morning without an appointment."

"You don't need a pastor to confess your sins to," I reminded him. "There are a lot of good churches in the area where you could have met with a member of their counseling staff as easily as you met with me."

"I know," he said. "For a problem like this I didn't want to talk to a counselor. Talking to a pastor was the only way for me to know how seriously I had to take this. Thanks for seeing me."

We shook hands and he left my office into a now-silent church hallway, the morning crowd having gone home. As I walked through the building, checking doors and lights, I smiled to myself.

Only in a Small Church, I thought.

There is no ideal church size. Every size meets the needs of the people who seek them out. But, while there are many things big churches can offer that Small Churches can't, there are also some things Small Churches can offer that big churches can't. Here are just a few.

My Pastor Knows My Name

As illustrated in the above story, only in a Small Church does everyone have direct access to the pastor.

Some people don't feel the need for such access, but many do. Many big- and megachurches have home groups that provide pastoral care for their members. But some people – most people, from what I've seen – prefer to receive pastoral care from the man or woman who preaches on Sundays. We can explain the ranching model of church growth to them until we're blue in the face, but most of them continue to have this strange, frustrating need to actually be pastored by their pastor.

It's one of the reasons I became a pastor to begin with. I don't want to be an administrator. I want to be available on Sundays. I don't want three layers of secretaries or associates between myself and a congregation member during the work-week. And I'm tired of being told that this desire means I'm somehow limiting God's work rather than doing God's work.

Many, I believe *most* people who attend a Small Church do so in large part because they want personal access to someone who can walk them through what it means to be a growing believer. Someone who will challenge them on a personal level because they're known on a personal level. They'll even put up with less-than-great preaching, second-rate musical skills, inadequate facilities or other Small Church issues if they know they can call someone who'll be personally available to advise, counsel, nudge or simply be there for them when they need spiritual nourishment or accountability.

I really believe in the priesthood of all believers. So I understand that my prayers as a pastor have no greater effect than any other believer's prayers. But I also know that leadership and calling matter. Because of that, it matters to many people that the pastor personally prays for them, counsels them and visits them in the hospital.

Many Christians receive all the spiritual nourishment they need in a large crowd with excellent amenities and superb Bible teaching while finding the personal touch in a home group or from a church staff counselor. But most Christians want to be led by the leader. They want to know they matter to the pastor.

I think this is one of the reasons most people who go to church attend a Small Church. It's not because they don't have better options. For example, there are at least half a dozen world-renowned megachurches within driving distance of our church building. But the people in my church come to listen to me every week. *Me*!

It's not because I'm the best preacher in the county. (I'm no slouch either). It's because when we run into each other in the grocery store, I know their name.

The Pastor as Church Member

I am a member of my church, not just its pastor.

The next time I have an issue that I need to talk through, I don't want to have to pay someone by the hour to be my friend. I want to talk to an actual friend in my church, like everyone else gets to do. Ranchers can't do that. Shepherds can.

This is my church too, and I want to be a part of all the joy, fun and friendship it has to offer. If I pastored a megachurch, I'd miss the opportunities I now have to hang out in the lobby with friends before and after church services or to high-five a group of guys I bunked with at the last men's retreat. It matters that when I tie the knot for a young couple I can smile at the bride's parents sitting proudly in the front row while the three of us remember the day we stood on that same stage to dedicate the bride when she was a baby.

In over 25 years of pastoral ministry I've talked with hundreds of fellow pastors about our mutual challenges in ministry. I've noticed that many big church pastors find their primary friendships among other big church pastors. That's understandable. Their lives intersect in many ways and they have a lot they can gain out of such relationships. But I've also noticed that they have to work that much harder to keep their spiritual footing because, the larger their church gets the less nurture they are able to receive from it themselves.

It's a real dilemma for big church pastors. The bigger the church, the more the pastoral role must change from personal shepherd to administrative oversight.

I was helped to understand this dilemma a couple years ago. At the 2010 West Coast Catalyst conference held at Mariner's Church in Irvine, California I was given a ticket from a fellow pastor to attend an exclusive lunch with Andy Stanley, the founder of Catalyst. It was a great opportunity to sit with about 30 others and ask Andy some personal questions.

In that setting, Stanley shared a story that, for me, illustrated one of the big differences between Small Church and big church philosophies.

Recently he'd been approached by a fairly new member of his church who was very persistent about wanting to schedule a personal sit-down with him. His response, as he told us, was to tell her that he wasn't able to have personal one-on-one times with church members because there were too many of them.

Then he told us that if he was ever asked a similar question again, he'd say that the reason he couldn't meet with her was the very reason she liked the church so much. Namely, the church had grown so big and meant so much to so many people because he dedicated his time to overseeing the staff ministries rather than taking care of each member's personal needs.

I get that. I appreciate the need for that.

But I couldn't do that.

That's nobody's fault. Not Stanley's, not mine. Because there's nothing wrong with it.

We all have different gift mixes. Some work best in one size of church, but not in another. Stanley's administrative style meets one set of needs, while my more hands-on style meets others.

Now don't get me wrong, I'll gladly accept any numerical growth that comes our way, and I'll do whatever adaptations are needed to allow and promote such growth. But I would also mourn the loss of something important if dramatic numerical growth happened – intimacy.

Intimacy and Accountability

Recently I was in the used book store of our community library when I overheard a conversation between two volunteers stacking shelves. As I walked by their aisle, these women had just realized that they both attended the same megachurch. The older woman said she'd been going there for decades, the younger one for a few years. The pastor had recently been ill and the previous Sunday had been his first weekend back in many months. The older woman expressed how much she'd missed him and how good it was to have him back preaching again.

"Did you tell him that?" her friend asked.

"Oh no. The church is so big now that no one can just walk up and talk to the pastor."

"True. It's a great church, but I've been going for years and don't really know anyone."

"If you want to know people you have to go to a small church."

There was a pause.

"Then you know *everyone*," said the younger lady.

"And they all know you," responded the older one.

They paused again while that last revelation hung in the air between them – and I tried to make myself look otherwise occupied nearby.

"So," said the older lady, picking up a stack of books, "where were these supposed to go again?"

They busied themselves with their work as if the prior conversation had never taken place.

Intimacy and accountability. Knowing and being known. Some people like it, some don't.

I like intimacy. I also like big events. My wife and I saw U2 in concert at the Rose Bowl a couple years ago. Part of the thrill of the evening was that we were in a crowd of over 120,000 watching a show on a spectacularly grand scale.

But when a crowd gets to a certain size, that's all it can be – a crowd. An audience.

You need a smaller group if you want intimacy. Most big churches offer that as an option. But in a Small Church it's unavoidable. Some people love that about Small Churches. Others don't because, as illustrated by the two women in the bookstore, that intimacy always comes with a flip-side – accountability. We all *need* both, but not all of us *want* both.

It's no surprise that some people go to big churches not just because of the excellence of the programs, but because they can be anonymous. They can attend without committing, receive without giving and slip in and out without getting to know anyone – or *being* known by anyone.

Many big churches have systems in place to offer people spiritual accountability. But in a big church you have to sign up for it. And many don't.

It's harder to do that in a Small Church. People miss you because the hole you leave is bigger. You get to know everyone, but that means everyone knows you, too.

When I look at our current culture and imagine it extending into the next 20, 30 or even 50 years, I see many people in our culture fleeing intimacy, like those two friends. But even more than that, I imagine there will be a parallel growing passion in people's hearts for true intimacy. If they can't find it in the church, they'll look elsewhere. Vibrant, healthy Small Churches have a window of opportunity in this next generational cycle to meet those needs like we've never seen before. If we miss that chance now, the door may close for a long time to come.

As a pastor, it's a powerful privilege to preach to faces you know. To people who were in your office in the past week confessing their sins, crying out for help or seeking wise counsel. People who have asked you to hold them accountable.

I've preached to larger groups, and I enjoy the opportunity to do so. But I've never been a megachurch pastor, looking out week after week at a sea of faces, most of whom I don't know personally. There's nothing wrong with that. It's just that my calling and my ministry finds a greater fulfillment – and it feels more like dialogue than monologue – when I know most of the names of the people in front of me.

Because I pastor a Small Church, I don't preach to a crowd, I preach to individuals. I know some very deep things about most of the people sitting in front of me. Some deep, dark things and some deep, wonderful things. While I don't bring up those intimate issues when I preach, the fact that I know them gives my messages a poignancy that can't exist in the most eloquent of messages preached to a nameless crowd or to people watching on a screen in another room or on the internet at home.

I have nothing against megachurches. I applaud any use of systems and technology that allow for a greater dissemination of the gospel. But we have to acknowledge that at some point along the scale from "the pastor knows my name" to "the pastor might be able to see me in the crowd" to "I can see the pastor's image on the screen, but he can't see me" to "I'll change channels or websites and watch a different pastor for a while" it stops being intimate.

At some point it also stops being *church,* doesn't it?

More Real Moments

As I write this, my wife and I are enjoying a beautiful Sunday afternoon at Lake Arrowhead, California. I came here for several days to get away and write a major portion of what you're currently reading. This morning Shelley and I went to a Small Church in town.

This church usually has a full band leading the worship service, but today their leader was sick, so another staff member grabbed a guitar to fill in, joined by one other vocalist. He asked us to pray for the Worship Leader, then told us that all he could do today was sing a few songs he knew, and he hoped we knew them too.

He led us in a few simple choruses and hymns. As predicted, we knew some, but not all of them. His co-singer on stage didn't seem to know them all, either. Everyone in the congregation felt like we were responsible to pitch in a little because of the unusual circumstances, so we did. Musically it wasn't what anyone came expecting, but his heart was right, he was a decent guitar player and singer, and that was good enough.

Spiritually however, it was something other than that. It was intimate. At times it was awkward. But that intimacy and awkwardness were part of what made it real. And that made it special.

Real moments like that don't happen very often in a big church because real moments are usually unintentional, and big churches seldom do anything unintentionally. Big churches have back-up plans, including back-up bands. And they should.

I've actually begun to distrust any church service that makes worship too easy for me. Worship should take some effort on my part, no matter who I am. No, I don't want a church service that *hinders* my worship experience, but it should *challenge* us, shouldn't it? I want to be a part of a worship experience that requires my participation rather than encouraging passivity.

Let's not sugar-coat this. Real moments in Small Churches don't always turn out as well as this one did. But in Small Churches they happen more often. That chance for authenticity, even when it's not so smooth and polished – maybe *because* it's not so smooth and polished – is a big part of what many people, especially younger people, crave in their lives and their worship experience.

A Longer Learning Curve

In big churches there's a high level of excellence required for people to serve, especially in areas of visible ministry – and rightfully so. So where do people at the beginning or in the middle of the learning curve get a chance to stretch and grow?

When I started pastoring my current church, excellence wasn't required from the ministry volunteers. Availability was all that was required. Competence was a bonus.

I came to a church with an average Sunday morning attendance of about 35 very discouraged people, over half of whom were seniors. Just prior to my arrival some of the leaders had debated taking a vote to close the doors.

The Youth Pastor was doing a good job with the kids during the week, but he was only a couple years out of High School and had little ministry education other than on-the-job-training. Very few of his youth could be convinced to come on Sunday mornings.

On stage were a piano and an organ that hadn't been touched in years because there was no one to play them. I promptly removed the organ before my first Sunday for fear that someone would walk in, see it and say, "I can play that for you!"

The church operated a thriving preschool on Monday through Friday, but not one child, parent or teacher from the preschool attended the church. I could go on, but you get the idea.

So I went to our denominational Bible College, just a ten-minute drive from the church, and I started recruiting. "No experience required" was the buzzword as I asked, encouraged, cajoled and begged my way around campus for several months. I talked with fresh young ministers-in-training about offering them a setting where they could test their skills in teaching, singing, playing an instrument, you name it. All I asked was as much commitment as they could offer while school was in session and a minimal level of competence. To my surprise, they showed up.

They came little by little at first, then in a massive flood when school started the following September. By "massive flood" I mean about 50 students, which doubled our congregation size overnight. Word had gotten out that there was a church near the school where they could try, fail, grow and get better in ministry while being loved through their inevitable mistakes.

We're told that we're supposed to strive for excellence and that God deserves nothing but our best. I've read that in virtually every church growth book and heard it at almost every pastoral ministry conference, just like you have. Yet if I had insisted on that standard for our church in those early days I have no doubt the church would no longer exist today.

It's a given that excellence is a moral imperative. But where, exactly does the Bible say that? Is it possible that we've elevated a biblically and morally neutral trait of *excellence* over a biblically essential trait of *obedience*?

I don't agree with the idea that God only wants our best. Just because a lot of people say something doesn't make it true.

When people say, "God deserves only the best," are they paying attention to the list of disciples Jesus picked?

Instead of a demand for excellence, I read in the Bible that God wants our *all*. Best, worst and everything in between. Maybe one of the finest things we can do, especially in Small Churches, is to provide a safe harbor for all those gifts to be offered and developed.

We often say things like, "God isn't looking for our ability, but our availability." I happen to believe he wants both. But if we're going to do more than pay lip service to the idea that availability matters, we need places where people with not much more than availability, passion and commitment can stretch those muscles and make mistakes in a loving environment. That has to be worth at least as much as a smooth-running weekend worship stage show, doesn't it?

Where else is that kind of talent going to be not just allowed and nurtured, but genuinely needed and applauded, than in a Small Church?

When we saw the initial mass of college students come in and overwhelm our older, small congregation, we decided that we would be a teaching church much like some hospitals are teaching hospitals. As a result we've had a lot of people pass through our doors who've picked up some valuable ministry experience and life-lessons while they were with us. Some stuck around long-term, but most have moved on. Many departed when they graduated. Some of them left because they got so good at doing ministry while they were with us that they got hired by bigger churches with bigger budgets.

As I write this I can easily recall the names of dozens of former students who barely knew how to get out of their own way the first time they sang on our church stage or stuttered their way through a home group teaching session, who are now ministering with excellence and passion in small, medium, big and megachurches across the country and around the world.

When you look at our Sunday attendance figures, that ministry approach may not have resulted in church growth. But make no mistake, it did result in the growth of the church.

Availability needs a training ground if it is going to become ability. Small Churches have been that training ground for millennia, and will continue to be so for as long as Christ continues building his church.

The next time you're in a big church, pause for a moment and consider this. As you're led by an inspiring worship leader, sit under excellent teaching or pick your child up from a top-notch Children's Ministries Department, be grateful that the church you're in is making that ministry available to you on a donation-only basis. Big churches are one of the few places in our culture still doing that without charge.

Then take a moment to thank a Small Church. That's likely where the people providing those ministries got their start.

Permission to Make Mistakes

During the interview process to become the pastor of the church I currently serve, they asked me what my vision was for the church and the community.

I told them I didn't have one.

As I explained (to a now very confused Pastoral Search Committee), it seemed presumptuous of me to say I had the answers for a church and a community I had spent less than a few hours in. I told them that if God called me to pastor their church, I would spend the first several years working with them to discover that vision.

It's been 20 years and I'm still here, so that answer must have worked.

The handful of people attending the church at the time were almost entirely seniors, but the community around them was mostly young families, including the one I would be bringing with me. I told them that if I became their pastor, life would immediately get messy and noisy. To attract younger people, which they said they wanted, we would be trying some things that might make some of the current members uncomfortable. Things might even get worse before they got better.

In the first few months I tried some events and strategies that thoroughly tested their mess and noise toleration limits (oh, who am I kidding? I've been testing those limits with them for the last two decades). A couple of those early ideas worked, but most failed miserably.

After one particularly spectacular failure, I knew the church leadership was going to chew me out. I went to the deacon board meeting with great apprehension. When we arrived at the point on the agenda to discuss my most recent calamity, I started to apologize. Before I could even get the first sentence out, I was interrupted by one of the deacons. "Pastor, stop," he said. *Oh boy,* I thought, *they're so angry they're not even going to let me get my apology out. I hope we saved some of those moving boxes.*

The deacon continued. "I know what you're going to say. It didn't go so well. But I think I speak for everyone here when I say we're grateful to see someone finally trying so hard on behalf of this church. You told us things wouldn't go smoothly at first, and you were right."

I laughed nervously. I was the only one who did.

"Pastor," he said as he leaned in to me, "we give you permission to make mistakes."

Have sweeter words ever been heard by a pastor at a board meeting? I think not. I couldn't have felt better if they'd offered to double my salary. Well, maybe a *little* better.

Obviously, not all Small Churches are so gracious. And I'm not saying that we ought to make a habit of making mistakes just because we can. Although I have taken full opportunity of that permission, I must admit. But only in Small Churches can months or years of trial-by-error even be a viable option.

Mistakes are too costly in big churches. Big churches are like big ships and big companies. Change often comes slowly because risks are too expensive to attempt without plenty of advance planning, focus-group confirmation and budget allocations.

Since I was given such grace that day, I have tried to pay it forward. I don't expect perfection from my staff or volunteers, I expect passion and commitment. I also let them know that anyone who ever tried something special or new made mistakes along the way. If you're not making mistakes, you're not growing.

There's an emotional and spiritual maturity that we can only gain from falling down, picking ourselves up and trying again. There's more room for that in a Small Church.

Meeting the Needs of Small Church People

Small Church People come in all shapes and sizes. They're not all backwards-looking hicks who want to stifle the growth of the church and keep things the way they've always been.

Some people just like going to a Small Church instead of a big church. That's where they find their greatest spiritual nourishment and a better chance to serve and grow.

Big and megachurches meet the needs of two kinds of people — big- and megachurch people. I'm grateful that they do. But as we're building our big churches let's not forget the needs of the rest of the population. The ones who feel lost in a crowd of over a couple hundred people. The ones who want to see familiar, friendly faces week after week.

These people aren't resistant to the arrival of new people, to evangelism or to the ministries of the church expanding and blessing their community. They simply find that their needs are met best, not in a cathedral or a former mini-mall, but in a little chapel, a converted bar or a storefront.

I was listening to a classic rock station the other day when John Mellencamp's *Small Town* came on the radio. I didn't expect to get anything profound from the guy who wrote "Hurt So Good," so I was quite surprised to hear that the familiar lyrics coming through my car stereo spoke as strongly as any teaching I've ever heard about why so many people like worshipping in a Small Church – not that this was Mellencamp's intention.

It's too expensive to buy the rights to reprint those lyrics here, but if you look them up online you'll see what I mean. Just take his lyrics celebrating small town life and replace "town" with "church". I'll do it for you with this excerpt: *"Educated in a small church. Taught to fear Jesus in a small church. … No I cannot forget where it is that I come from. I cannot forget the people who love me. Yeah, I can be myself here in this small church…"*

It's interesting that most people are OK with a celebration of life in a small town. But if you want to have the benefits of a Small Church, many will label you a vision-killer.

The Next Church (or World) Revolution

If the church is ever going to have a new Reformation, the spark for it will almost surely be provided by a Small Church or a network of Small Churches. It is very unlikely to come from a big church or a denomination. This discovery is one of the biggest reasons I have become such a cheerleader for New Small Churches.

Revolution never happens by getting the best, brightest, most successful people together. When that happens, watch your wallets and your freedoms. When the powerful join forces, they never do so to change the status quo. The simple fact of their success means the current system is working for them, so why would they want to change it?

The American Revolution is a great example of that. Today when we see the glorious depictions of George Washington, Alexander Hamilton, Benjamin Franklin and others in Independence Hall for the Constitutional Convention, we think, "they were the best and brightest. And they started one of the world's great revolutions." But that meeting was only so grand in hindsight – and only because they won. At the time, they were a motley group of mostly farmers, merchants and tradesmen. The smart and powerful were all in London.

Revolution has always come, and will always come from the poor, the small, the under-represented and under-appreciated. As a part of that motley band, Small Churches and their leaders have played a central role in more of the world's great revolutions than most of us realize.

The founding of America had Small Churches at its core, all the way from the band of Pilgrims who left England for religious freedom, escaping a corrupt government and its compatriots in a politically compromised, patriarchal big church system. Let's not forget that 37 of the 102 passengers on the Mayflower were members of Netherland's Leiden congregation – a Small Church.

Starting with that Small Church, much of the impetus for the growth of America up to and beyond the American Revolution came through the theology, relationships and sermons of churches, most of which were small.

Most of the great drives for freedom in America were started and/or sustained through Small Churches. The eventual overturn of slavery was sparked in Small Churches and, until the Emancipation Proclamation freed the slaves, Small Churches provided many of the vital links in the Underground Railroad that ferried runaway slaves to freedom.

Later on, the right of women to vote was largely sparked by sermons, and these were usually preached from the pulpits of Small Churches. The Civil Rights Movement of the 1960s was led by Rev. Dr. Martin Luther King Jr., the pastor of a small congregation called Ebenezer Baptist church.

In the early 1900s it was a Small Church pastor named William Seymour who launched the Pentecostal revival from a 60ft x 40ft building on Azusa Street in downtown Los Angeles that one local newspaper referred to as a "tumble down shack".

It's not just an American phenomenon, either. Revolutions around the world have been inspired by God's hand at work in Small Churches – sometimes almost invisibly.

The story of St. Patrick is rife with myths and legends, but when you strip it back to what we can know for sure what we find is that he planted dozens, possibly hundreds of Small Churches that changed Ireland and the world.

John Wesley's Methodist revival started with the training and sending of teams of circuit-riding preachers who rode from town-to-town on horseback, pastoring several Small Churches at a time on a rotating basis, as did Wesley himself. The key to the Wesleyan revival and subsequent growth is widely credited to his accountability system, in which the groups were intentionally kept very small.

Dietrich Bonhoeffer and the tiny Confessing Church movement are rightfully lauded for their opposition to Adolf Hitler while larger churches and denominations were making concessions to the Nazis.

In 1989, the Berlin Wall fell. It is now universally acknowledged that prayer meetings in illegal Small Churches were one of the critical catalysts that led to it.

Then, in December of that year, the Romanian Revolution was set ablaze when Romanian dictator Nicolae Ceaușescu ordered that László Tőkés be removed from his position as Associate Pastor of his Small Church in Timişoara due to Tőkés' vocal opposition to the brutal regime. Tőkés' parishioners surrounded his home to protect him from government forces, and the ensuing protests and riots spread quickly throughout the nation leading to the arrest, trial and execution of the Ceauşescus before the month was over.

In Europe especially, I'm convinced that if a spiritual renewal is going to happen it will need to be through a network of Small Churches. With Europe's history of oppression and corruption at the hands of powerful ecclesiastical forces, an emergence of megachurches or a re-emergence of large cathedrals will be met with great suspicion and fear – and justifiably so. A New Small Church grass-roots movement is the only way post-Christian Europe is going to perceive a renewal of Christianity as a genuine spiritual movement, rather than a political strategy.

Revolutions always need a spark to fire them up. Who is the next László Tőkés, William J. Seymour or Martin Luther King Jr.? What will ignite the next church Reformation? I don't know, but history tells us it's far more likely to come from a Small Church – or a united group of Small Churches – than a megachurch.

Chapter 8

Small Church, Big Vision

New Small Church is not about timid little churches.

It's not about pastors and leaders who operate out of guilt or fear. It's not about congregations that don't want to move forward. It's definitely not about settling for less.

It *is* about discovering who we are as churches, leaders and congregations, then using that newfound knowledge to be what God has called us to be in fresh, new ways. Including discovering the wonderful advantages that come with being small.

Small Churches need to think like Small Churches.

But *thinking small* is not the same as *small thinking*. And it's definitely not an excuse for having a small vision.

For the last few decades the western church has been focused on how to turn a big vision into a big church. Has that focus blinded us to the possibility that we can operate with a big vision in a Small Church? If so, could we recognize one if we saw it?

What does a Small Church with big vision look like?

Discovering and living that is what the New Small Church is all about.

No two churches are alike, of course. But I'd like to offer some observations from my experiences in Small Churches, my discussions with Small Church pastors, and my years of thought and prayer about this.

Here are some characteristics that Small Churches with big visions will likely have in common.

Forget Your Troubles, Come On Get Healthy

I spent too many years trying to place blame for my and my church's failures – both real and imagined – on others.

I blamed my pastoral predecessors because they under-bought and under-built.
If only they'd had more faith and bought more land, then I wouldn't be in this mess.

I blamed demographic shifts in the community.
We live where people are in transition. It's hard to gain momentum and maintain growth.

I blamed my college professors.
They left out some of the most important lessons of pastoral ministry, didn't they?

I blamed the people who *were* coming for the people who *weren't* coming.
Then I wondered why they left too?

Then I looked around and saw other churches with all those challenges and more, but many of them were growing like crazy.

So I turned to the only place left to blame.

I blamed myself.

I'm not working hard enough.
I'm not applying the right principles in the right way.
I'm not in the right church/town/type of ministry to fulfill my calling.
I'm not good enough.
I missed God's call.

When I finally got a healthy perspective on myself and my ministry I realized none of those excuses were valid.

As it turns out, many of my failures ... *weren't*.

I used to think that the reason my church wasn't getting big under my leadership was because "I'm just not that good."

As it turns out, "I'm just not ... *that*."

I had to forget about the things I'm *not* and start appreciating the things I *am*.

Healthy churches do not grow under the guidance of disgruntled, demoralized pastors. One of the primary reasons for writing my story was to help other Small Church pastors do what it took me too many years to do – stop being upset about what I'm *not* and start discovering and enjoying who I *am*.

We need to stop using numerical growth as the primary indicator of success in ministry and start looking at *health* as the primary indicator of success in ministry. It may all start with this premise – a healthy church that's not growing numerically is better than an unhealthy church that is.

When Cornerstone grew to over 350 in Sunday attendance (almost 450 with kids) it was no longer a Small Church. But it was far less healthy, and certainly less health*ful* to the community and the world than it is today at under 200 in Sunday attendance (pushing 250 with kids). That ill-health is one of the main reasons the growth could not be sustained.

I'm grateful that God did not allow me to succeed in the path I was on, with so much energy focused on pushing to some self-imposed next level, instead of being who we are.

There are plenty of factors that go into becoming a healthy church and they are not easy to define. I think the main reason we use numerical growth as our primary indicator is that numbers are easier to assess than healthfulness.

Perhaps no other factor is a better starting point for the health of a church – and certainly for the spiritual health of pastors – than the words of the Apostle Paul about contentment.

> But godliness with contentment is great gain. (1 Timothy 6:6)

> I have learned to be content whatever the circumstances. I know what it is to be in need, and I know what it is to have plenty. I have learned the secret of being content in any and every situation, whether well fed or hungry, whether living in plenty or in want. I can do everything through him who gives me strength. (Philippians 4:11-13)

Who are you? What has God called you to do? Can you be content with that?

Philippians 4:13 has probably been quoted out of context more than any other verse in the Bible. It's not telling us we can do *everything we want*. ("I *can* build a megachurch in a town of 5,000 through him who gives me strength!"). If we start with the context of verse 11, it's clear that Paul is telling us that God wants to give us the strength to be *content* in any situation.

That's Step One to becoming a healthy pastor and a healthy church

– being content with how God made you and what he called you to do and be.

We tell our congregation members to be happy with the role God gave them. That taking out the trash or setting up chairs is as essential to helping a church run as preaching or singing on stage. But do we really believe it? If we did, we'd be OK with the less-than-glamorous pastoral tasks God calls most of us to do for much of our ministry years.

Very few pastors are actually called by God to work in large settings among wealthy people with huge, almost limitless resources. Most of us are asked to dig in with the poor and disheartened, with limited space, money and resources. That's where Jesus and most of the early apostles spent the bulk of their time, so why should we expect different? According to the passage I just quoted, Paul had his share of both, and found that Christ gave him the strength to meet the challenges of each.

When I say we need to be content, it may raise some red flags for you. For a lot of people, contentment (again) sounds like settling and settling sounds like giving up. Nothing could be further from the truth.

Biblical contentment is never an excuse for settling. *not complacency* Contentment can't be "great gain" without the accompanying godliness. Giving up is never godly.

Let's face facts – there are plenty of Small Churches that are smaller than they ought to be because of incompetence, laziness, self-righteousness and a variety of other symptoms. We've all seen too many cases of mediocrity in pastors that have caused us to say, "no wonder that church is so small".

That's not contentment. That's complacency. Sometimes it's laziness, corruption, incompetence, stubbornness, selfishness… the list goes on. There's no contentment or godliness in any of that.

We need to be content with *who* we are, <u>but never content with staying *where* we are</u>. I'm not a fan of bromides like "be the best possible you, you can be!" but I have realized that it's only after discovering who I *am* and who I am *not* in Christ, that I can be set free to do and be what God made me to do and be.

If we're not content with who we are, no amount of church growth will bring that contentment. If we are content, we'll be spurred on from the resulting hope and joy to do great things for God, our church and the community, no matter what size church we pastor.

Reach the Community You're In by Pastoring the Church You Have

In the lead-up to the second Gulf War, Secretary of Defense Donald Rumsfeld found himself in trouble by his awkwardly timed and fumblingly stated quote "As you know, you go to war with the Army you have. They're not the Army you might want or wish to have at a later time."

Some church growth proponents have made a similar mistake. When they teach the "think like a big church" philosophy, I've heard some say, "what I mean by that is, pastor the Church you *want* to have."

There are numerous problems with pastoring the church you *want* to have, instead of the church you've *got*. Primarily, the church you've got usually gets left out of the equation and isn't pastored properly.

The reason people were so upset with Secretary Rumsfeld's statement was that it sounded like he was putting down the American military as an inadequate fighting force. When we say similar things about what we *wish* our church was, we can demoralize them in the same way.

Instead, I have learned that the best way to utilize what we've been given is to appreciate and pastor the church we've got.

By that, I do not mean that we should be limiting ourselves to just the people who show up for weekend worship. For instance, during my struggle to grow a big church I made one decision correctly. We were looking for a new church building to meet in and we heard that another church in the area was looking for a buyer for their current building. It was a beautiful facility in so many ways. The main auditorium was triple our current size, and the classrooms, lobby and offices were spacious and smart without being ornate or flashy.

I turned it down for two reasons: first, it was in the middle of an industrial park about five miles from our current building. The realtor correctly pointed out that a five mile drive wasn't far in our area, and that our current Sunday morning congregation would easily follow us there. I agreed that was probably true. We'd actually be closer to some of our current members in this building than we were in our current one.

But if we moved five miles away we would lose out on ministering to hundreds of families in the community with whom we'd been building relationships. The people we had in the church already, we'd keep. The people we were working with in the neighborhood, we'd lose. We'd invested too much time and passion into those burgeoning relationships to walk away from them. Those people mattered to us, and we mattered to them.

Secondly, relocating to an industrial park would mean that any future growth wouldn't come from the new neighborhood, since there wasn't one, but would more likely be transfer growth from other churches. In the new location the only people who would come to the church were people who already knew where to find us – and that would almost exclusively be church people, not the unchurched.

We could have moved. We might have even grown. It might have become a really good church in that new location. That had certainly happened for the church which previously occupied the building. But it wouldn't have been the *same* church. And God didn't call me to pastor *that* church, he called me to pastor *this* one.

Too often we make the mistake, in church growth circles, of only counting the ministry we do in weekend worship services. In our new location, we'd have maintained that growth, and possibly even increased it, but when you factor in the neighborhood families we'd have lost contact with, I'm convinced the real number of people we provide weekly ministry to would have actually dropped, even if our weekend worship attendance grew.

It's a trade I was not, and am not willing to make.

Not a Miniature Big Church

One of the biggest mistakes I see in Small Churches is when we try to act like a big church, just on a smaller scale. That is not big vision thinking.

A red grape isn't a miniature plum. They may have many things in common, including their color and shape, but they each have their own distinct taste and set of nutrients. A grape that tries to act like a plum would make a lousy Christmas pudding, and it would miss out on the possibility of being in a bottle of wine that's used for a celebration of the Lord's Table.

A Small Church isn't a miniature big church. Small Churches have our own distinct taste and nutrients. A Small Church that tries to act like a big church will miss out on all the great things that only a Small Church can do.

This misguided act-like-a-big-church thinking has led to the following sad scene being repeated in thousands of Small Churches around the world. You walk into a weekend worship service and see a handful of people, seated in rows, often separated by huge spaces, while a worship director or pastor sings or preaches as though there were 1,000 people in the room. They look above people's heads instead of into their eyes as they talk *at* them instead of _to them_ (or, better yet, _with_ them).

Why do they *do* that? Because they think that's how it's done in a big church – and they mistakenly believe it to be a basic ingredient in getting their church to be big too.

We lose intimacy in a big church. Some of that can't be helped. But what a shame it is to give up intimacy in a Small Church when it should be one of our strongest assets.

Even though there are no megachurches in my town, the church I pastor is surrounded by some of the world's most famous megachurches in adjoining cities. On any weekend, anyone in my congregation can drive to the original Calvary Chapel or Vineyard, to Saddleback Church, the former Crystal Cathedral, Church on the Way, Angelus Temple, or even the TBN headquarters, not to mention dozens of other megachurches without international reputations.

Years ago we decided on two things in regard to those churches: first, we are not in competition with each other, and second, we would not try to be smaller-version duplicates of them. Trying to teach like Chuck Smith when people can hear the actual Chuck Smith less than ten minutes from our front door is not what God put us here to do.

So here's what we did. We decided to find out what we could do that no one else was doing. Then we did it. That's been our identity ever since.

There have been times when we've started a particular ministry to fill an obvious need in the community, only to see other churches start doing it a while later – sometimes better than us. In most of those cases, as soon as another church got strong in that ministry, we realized our time with that ministry was done, so we stopped doing it and started looking for other areas of need that no one else was filling.

That's us. We're starters. When others pick it up, we leave it to them and move on. It's not that we have to be original and cool. Most of the ideas we've introduced were concepts we borrowed from churches outside our area. We aren't more creative than others, we just don't see the need to duplicate what others in the neighborhood are already doing. One of the advantages of being small is that we can start and stop ministries quickly.

We also discovered that we were really good at training students and sending them off better prepared for life. So we started an internship program, run by my associate, Gary Garcia. Every year for about a decade now, four to six college-age students come from all around the world to live, work, worship and train with us from September through June. Others give up summer vacations.

Because of our size, they are able to learn hands-on leadership through experience instead of a classroom. When they're done, 90% of them move back home to bless their churches and communities.

Many Small Churches spend a lower percentage of their gross income on direct ministry than big churches. Some of that has to do with the systems efficiency and tighter management in big churches. But I wonder how much of the inefficiency of Small Churches is due to trying to think and act like a big church instead of appreciating and using our current size to its fullest advantage?

Is it possible that simply accepting our size and using the advantages it affords may be the single biggest step towards releasing thousands of local churches to be healthy and successful?

The Best Defense...

Most of the best ministries we start at Cornerstone happen when we do one critical thing: stop acting in fear and step out with boldness. Fear keeps more churches on the defense than anything else. A defensive church can't do anything but hang on for dear life to what it's got – until it usually loses that too.

Several years ago we re-tarred our old, weathered church parking lot. The tar had barely dried on it when we started hearing a commotion outside. Local teens were showing up to skateboard on the smooth new surface.

That's right. Teenagers just showed up, hanging around a church parking lot, thinking they had the right to use it as their own personal playground. We had a choice to make. Did they have that right, or didn't they? Was the building built to welcome the community or keep it out? Do we put up signs to keep them out, or do we find skateboard ramps to invite them in?

Churches on defense put up signs. Churches on offense put up ramps.

That was one of the defining moments of our church's history. Not only do we still have the only skateboard park in the city, but those ramps and the attitude behind them have set the tone for everything we've done ever since.

Grab the opportunities when God gives them to you.

Determine that the church building is going to serve the ministry, not *vise versa*.

Build ramps, even if it costs you more parking spaces and liability insurance than you think you can afford. What you get in return is of far greater – literally eternal – value.

Since the day we chose ramps over signs, hundreds, maybe thousands of kids have come to what they call Skate Church to have fun, make friends and hear about Jesus. Many of them have made commitments to follow Christ. Some of their families have followed. Several of them are in our church on Sundays now, while many are worshiping and serving God in dozens of other churches.

Small Church pastors like to complain that many big churches have given up passion for competence, but on the other side, many Small Churches have given up innovation for survival – offense for defense.

No one scores goals on defense.

And ramps are more fun than signs.

Think People, not Buildings

The church is not a building. We know that is true theologically, but pastors often behave in ways that teach the opposite.

Let's start with the budget. How many congregations around the world don't have money "left over" for ministry because so much of it is going into the maintenance of a historic building – even if the "history" is just in their own minds? In a Small Church especially, the mortgage can chew up a massive percentage of the budget. When the building takes that much priority, our budget dictates our theology.

How many churches feature a picture of their building as the central point of our logos, our bulletins and our websites? When we do so, we send a message. That message is, "this building is the church." I'm not saying it's wrong to use the image of a church building, of course. I've done it myself in the New Small Church logo. Church buildings have their place as a drawing-place for worship, and they need to be maintained properly. But when we put the building front and center, our marketing choices dictate our theology.

Soon we're debating whether-or-not we can do the ministry God laid out for us because it might clutter up the parking lot with cigarette butts or get the carpets dirty from so many kids tromping through. God forgive us when our janitorial schedule dictates our theology.

Buildings cost money. More of that money should be invested in people and less of it in buildings. Small Churches can get by with smaller or even no permanent facilities if we can allow ourselves to think that way. Let's make choices about our buildings, or lack thereof, which leverage the advantages of our small size. God will be blessed by that and so will the people God has called us to serve.

Better Use of Our Limited Resources

In a recent meeting of pastors, a panel of younger ministers was leading the group in a discussion of Dan Kimball's book, *They Like Jesus, but Not the Church.* I was looking forward to hearing from this panel because I really like Kimball's book.

At one point, the panel discussion was centered on a statement to Dan Kimball from a nonchristian friend, "I wish the church weren't all about the building." The panel proposed that one reason the unchurched and newly churched don't give as much money as previous generations is because they don't trust that the church is using their money well. They want to see more of it going into direct ministry to people instead of maintaining its physical structures.

One of the pastors in the audience responded, "Don't they realize that's hard to do? 90% of what they give is needed to pay for buildings, salaries and maintenance. They don't expect the majority of the money they give to go into *actual ministry* do they?" I thought he was being sarcastic and almost laughed out loud – *with* him, I assumed. Then I realized that most of the room was "amen-ing" him. Responses came in rapid-fire agreement. "They know it's that way for other businesses and institutions, but it's not OK for us?" was a typical response.

That's right. They don't think it's OK for us because it's *not* OK for us. We have a higher standard. Or we should. Everyone, both in and outside the church has the right – no, not just the right, the *duty* – to call us on it when we fall so obviously short of that standard.

They get it. Do we?

In both small and big churches we can be better stewards if we do what we're called to do instead of wasting resources on buildings, maintenance and structures that sometimes act as roadblocks instead of stepping stones.

Different Sized Missions for Different Sized Churches

Years ago I was at a pastoral conference where we were told (incorrectly) that Coca-Cola's mission statement was, "to put a Coca-Cola into the hands of every person on earth". The point was that if Coca-Cola could be that excited and successful at marketing colored sugar-water, we ought to be at least as excited and successful at marketing a product of infinitely greater value. Our dreams for the church should be at least as big as Coca-Cola's.

Aside from my growing revulsion at using words like *marketing* and *product* in the context of bringing people to a growing relationship with Jesus, you may be surprised to find that I agree with that premise – to an extent.

Such a pervasive, global reach is the mission of *The* Church. Jesus said so when he told us to, "Go into all the world and preach the good news to all creation." That's at least as comprehensive as Coca-Cola's supposed mission statement. But it's the mission of the *entire* church, not of every *individual* church.

Not every church has a Coca-Cola sized mission. Some have a Jones Soda sized mission.

Jones Soda is sometimes thought of as the anti-Coke brand. They don't intend or expect to put their product into the hands of everyone on earth. Instead, they've carved out a niche to meet a need no one else is meeting. If you've never heard of Jones Soda, they're a plucky little company famous for two things: unique flavors like Strawberry-Lime, Fufu Berry and even holiday flavors like Turkey (yes, turkey soda!), and for putting photos of their customers on their bottles.

Jones Soda will never be huge. They'll never cause a moment of lost sleep at Coca-Cola headquarters. That's OK with them. The people who like Jones Soda are *very* passionate about it. And no one can say they haven't been successful at what they set out to do.

To use another business-oriented illustration, not every restaurant is going to be the size of McDonald's or the quality of a five-star fine dining experience. Nor should they be, because not everyone likes chain restaurants and even fewer can afford fine dining. The world needs cafés, bistros and greasy spoons. Places that meet the needs of the locals, speak the language of the community and inspire other young restaurateurs to open their own establishments.

There's a restaurant in New York City named Rao's (RAY-os) that has just ten tables. For generations Rao's has been one of the most influential and respected Italian restaurants on earth. Their recipes and innovations have inspired untold numbers of chefs around the world who have gone on to feed and delight the palates of perhaps millions of diners. All from a restaurant that still has only ten tables.

In the same way, the megachurch model isn't the only model of church ministry. The megachurch model works for megachurches. That's less than 1% of the churches in the world. But it's the only model we regularly hear or read about. That has to change.

The world only has room for a limited number of megachurches built on a mission like Coca-Cola's. But the sky's the limit on how many Small Churches can have an impact like Rao's restaurant. Small size, huge impact. I'd like to think that my church can be one of them. Actually, I know my church is one of them. And we're not the only one. We're not even the only one in my town. There are a lot of high-impact Small Churches out there that very few of us know about.

We need more megachurches in the world – at least a few more. We need more Small Churches too – a *lot* more.

A Reputation Bigger Than the Facility

The church I pastor ministers to people, touches our community and reaches around the world in extraordinary ways. Despite that, we are probably never going to be a big church.

But we have a big reputation.

Because of the kind of ministry we do and the big vision we have, people who visit our church facility are often shocked when I show them around the building. People have actually asked me when I was going to show them the main sanctuary *while we were standing in the main sanctuary!* It's so small, they assumed we were in the prayer chapel. "This is all the facility we have" I told them. I used to be embarrassed to admit that. Now it cracks me up. I love it.

We're bigger than our building.

The main chapel of our church building is the very definition of a multi-use room. On special occasions we can seat 175, but that is *very* full. A couple times we've jammed in as many as 230 in by reducing the aisles to almost zero and with people standing around the edge and in the outer hallway.

But it's by far the biggest room we have, so we use it a lot. In an average week we set it up and break it down nine or ten times. On a busy week, more than a dozen times.

I'm deeply grateful for the small army of volunteers and staff members who do this work every week with joyful, willing hearts. I admit I still get frustrated by the restrictions of our small building. Believe me, I wouldn't turn down a larger building if we had a good chance at getting one. But those frustrations pale beside the joy I have in knowing that we're using what we've got in fresh, innovative ways. And those are just the ministries that happen inside the chapel! We've also learned to use the rest of the building in creative ways, and we have plenty of ministries that don't depend on our facility at all.

Our church building may be small, but our vision, our ministry and our reputation doesn't have to be.

Be Who You Are – And Keep the Back Door Open

Small Churches that are great tend to be small *and* great for the same reason. They've figured out who they are and they're focused on doing that one thing well. Such a focused, passionate "one thing" mentality is often the very factor that will both fuel its success *and* enforce a cap on its numerical growth.

It will fuel its success, because that kind of focused passion will attract others who have a similar passion. But it will also cap that growth because it will automatically exclude those who don't share that passion, thus limiting its possibility for numerical growth. The New Small Church isn't trying to be everything for everyone.

Yet another mistake I believe many Small Church pastors make, and it's certainly one that I made, is to give in to the temptation to add to or abandon your "one thing" in order to grow numerically. It's not that our focus should never change as time goes on, but I do believe that betraying your focus and yourself merely to get the numbers up is a downward trade-off.

In a dynamic New Small Church, it's likely that many, even most of the people who visit any particular worship service won't understand or like what you're doing. That's been the case at Cornerstone for years. Our front door is welcoming, but our back door is open too. We know not everyone will like what we do and we're OK with that.

Our church is very active and informal, the fellowship is boisterous, teenagers roam freely, tattoos and piercings are common. Some people who visit the church are expecting something more churchy, so when they see all this going on before the service they get a bit uncomfortable, even though they're usually greeted warmly. The service starts and people settle in. The worship is fresh, new and lively, so some new folks start settling in with an appreciation for the relaxing vibe, while others are wondering how a church can possibly allow the band members to wear anything from jeans to shorts, T-shirts to dresses, running shoes to flip-flops.

At about the halfway point in the service, we have a coffee break. We believe that hanging out is holy (you may know it as fellowship), so we make it a part of the actual worship experience. The fact that people are encouraged to take five minutes to grab a donut and coffee, wander around chatting then come back to their seat chomping on a cruller is the tipping point for some people. It's also an opportunity. While they would never be rude enough to get up and walk out of a church service while everyone was sitting and paying quiet attention, it's very easy to slip out while people are chatting, drinking and eating. So they head to their car and drive off, wondering how what they've just experienced can be called church.

We aren't intentionally trying to drive people away, of course, but we also know that no church can make everyone happy. If what I've just described is the kind of thing that would send you to your car, that's fine. Most of the people in my church would probably drive away just as quickly from a church where people wear a suit and tie, sing hymns and listen to a robe-wearing choir. To each their own.

We feel no need to make people suffer through something they're not going to like, even if we like it, so we give them an easy out. They don't need to stick around if what we do isn't working for them. Besides, if they leave at the coffee break there's the added bonus that it wasn't my preaching that drove them out, right?

When you focus on being who you are without worrying about who doesn't like it, a lot of people won't like it. But those who do like it will be completely sold on it. The people who like what we do, *really* like it. Many have asked where this kind of church has been all their lives. When they're that enthused, they commit their heart and soul to its mission.

You may not grow a big church that way, but when you and your congregation are comfortable in your own skin and are following the way God is leading you, the result will be a great church. You'll be less stressed and more effective than ever, whether big numbers materialize or not.

To adapt a quote from Gil Bailie, "Don't ask yourself what the world needs. Ask yourself what makes you (and your church) come alive, and go do that, because what the world needs is more people (and churches) that have come alive." (Words in parentheses added by me)

New Generation Needs

In recent years, many megachurches have expanded their ministries by offering multiple venues either on- or off-site, with different styles of worship at each one. Such a church may have adult contemporary worship in their main auditorium, while in other venues they offer country music, alternative, traditional, etc., with worship sessions timed to end when the pastor is ready to preach live in the main hall linked to video screens in those other venues.

That's great. I've attended a couple of those churches and have enjoyed the chance to choose a different setting for worship. But some people just don't like a big campus vibe no matter how many worship styles you offer them.

In *They Like Jesus but Not the Church,* Dan Kimball relates some of the feelings new generations of non-believers have about Jesus and the church. The main result is reflected in the title, of course, but other findings were interesting too. One young woman expressed her desire for a church that was smaller and more intimate. As she so beautifully put it, "Make church a book club with soul." She's not alone in that longing.

Another unchurched friend of Kimball's told him, "...I think the meetings should be smaller. Every once in a while a big meeting is cool, but not as the norm." Yet another asked, "Didn't Jesus spend most of his time in smaller settings, with smaller groups? ... I bet that is where they learned the most from him, not when he was in the masses with larger crowds."

Some of what younger generations want and need from the church has nothing to do with the style of the worship band. Many of them just don't like the corporate vibe of a bigger church. What speaks to their heart can only happen in a smaller setting.

"Hey Grandma, I'll Save You a Seat!"

Yet another byword within the church growth movement was homogeneity – the concept that you can build a bigger church if everyone in it shares common characteristics. Based on this principle, pastors and church leaders around the world have sat down to decide, "this is the kind of person our church is trying to reach". Sometimes they draw a picture or take a photo of their "target" and give him or her a name. Then they design the messages, advertising, programs and the building itself to give that person what they're looking for.

In many cases it seems to work. People with similar lifestyles, backgrounds, needs and socio-economic status are drawn to a place that gives them just what they're looking for. When everyone gathers, even though they don't know each other, they're sitting next to people who look a lot like themselves.

Small Churches are usually more *hetero*geneous. Young and old sit side-by-side because the church doesn't have a youth service happening at the same time as the main service. Rich and poor get to know each other in the lobby. Long-time believers and not-yet believers discuss topics together because there aren't enough new people, or an extra classroom, to hold a weekly class just for seekers.

Small Churches make do without some conveniences and they often lack the quality control that big church attenders have come to expect. But what Small Churches lose in customer service they gain in relationships because Small Churches allow us, (OK *force* us, sometimes by nothing more than physical proximity) to get to know people who *aren't* the same as us.

Worshipping only with people who look like us is not healthy or biblical.

The early church was the first movement in history to reverse the societal requirement that slaves and free, Jews and gentiles, men and women, rich and poor had to live, eat, work and worship separately. When first-century churches of less than one hundred people gathered in homes to worship, fellowship and share the Lord's Table, the lines of gender, ethnicity and social status were erased. The church was the first societal structure *ever* to do this. It seems counter-intuitive that we could ever have another spiritual renewal without that being a central part of it again.

"Go Into…" and "Come and See"

In the late 1990s I started noticing something new for sale in Starbucks. In addition to coffee, they were selling games. Specifically, a fun-looking game called *Cranium.* In 2001 it was named Game of the Year and since then Cranium Inc. has had two more of their products named Game of the Year.

So what does selling games at Starbucks have to do with Small Churches? Several years ago, when advertising guru Donny Deutsch had his own cable TV show, I stumbled upon an interview he did with *Cranium* co-founder Whit Alexander. Deutsch's show was an exploration of entrepreneurship, so he was asking Alexander about Cranium's start, specifically why they decided to sell their game in Starbucks (and Amazon.com and Barnes & Noble) instead of traditional game stores or in the game departments of stores like Target and Wal-Mart.

Alexander's answer was simple. "We decided, let's take the games to where the people are, rather than where games are sold."

Brilliant. I'll resist the temptation to say that these guys really used their cranium.

In the Bible, people came to faith in Jesus in two ways. First, after Jesus asked Philip to follow him, Philip ran to recruit Nathanael. Nathanael was skeptical, so Philip said three words to convince him, "Come and see." Second, when Jesus told the disciples they had a duty to share their faith with others he told them to "Go into all the world and preach the good news to all creation."

"Go into…" and "Come and see".

Throughout church history we have used both strategies. But it's safe to say that we have leaned far more on the "Come and see" model than "Go into…". Missionaries may go into a particular culture, but the end game is usually to gain enough momentum to set up a tent or build a chapel. Then they send word out to the people to "Come and see" what's happening inside the confines of what's been built. "Go into…" fades into the background, while "Come and see" predominates.

That is certainly what 90% of the North American and European church culture has become. We construct buildings, hold concerts or advertise our Easter services. We put church things where church things are supposed to be and ask people to "Come and see".

Cranium knew something the church needs to re-learn. When you sell games where games are sold, game people show up, but few others do. When you put church things in churchy places, church people show up, but few others do.

By putting their games in Starbucks stores instead of game stores or game departments, *Cranium* sold far more than anyone thought they would, and mostly to people who never expected to buy a game. They created new game customers when they decided to "Go into…" an existing culture instead of sitting in a pre-built subculture and asking people to "Come and see" what they had to offer.

Small Churches can go into another culture. It's one of the advantages of being small. We can take church to the places non-church people are.

For example, several years ago, after having a couple rough pastoral experiences in big churches, Norb Kohler (who happens to be my brother-in-law) was standing in front of the fountain next to a multiplex theater in a new outdoor mall when he felt an internal nudge. *What would it be like to bring the church here instead of expecting the people here to come to us?* he wondered. He and my sister Kathy started talking and praying. Then they called others to talk and pray some more. To make a long story short, today their church, Convergence OC (OC for Orange County) has become a part of the culture of that mall.

Their Sunday services start next to the fountain where Norb felt that first nudge. People hang out for about half an hour, chatting, drinking coffee and eating snacks. Eventually they drift in to one of the theaters for a short talk from Norb, after which they close with some worship together. People who come to see a movie that day will look at the digital marquee and see the latest movie listed on one screen, with Convergence OC listed in the theater next to it.

During the week, Norb spends a lot of his ministry hours, not in the church office, because he doesn't have one, but hanging out with store and restaurant workers, managers and owners. By doing so, he's become the unofficial chaplain for a large suburban shopping mall. Store workers who have never attended a church service have told him they consider him to be their pastor – and he is.

When my niece, Natalie, became touched by the plight of young girls being sold into slavery throughout Asia, she started raising funds for ministries that literally buy people their freedom. Instead of asking church people to "Come and see" what this ministry was doing, she and the church went into the mall with it. They gathered around the fountain, brought baked goods and sold all-you-can-eat tickets for a $10 donation to people who had intended to come to the mall just to shop or watch a movie.

When restaurants in the mall heard what was happening, they offered to help, sending their employees out to walk around with trays of free samples. Our church loved the idea so much that we joined them, along with other small local congregations, to sponsor the next year's event. So for the past two years, in the middle of a suburban mall, people from several Small Churches and under-the-radar ministries have mixed with movie goers, shoppers and on-the-clock restaurant employees to eat, meet, chat and donate money to save the lives of young girls on the other side of the world.

Yes, big churches have an impact on a culture, but once a church reaches a certain size it loses its ability to invade a culture so much as it creates an alternative subculture. Big churches can't slide into the culture of a shopping mall. Big churches *buy* shopping malls and turn them into Christian-only zones. That has a value. But it's not the only thing we're called to do.

Big churches usually do "Come and see" ministry really well. For example, in order to have enough land to build on, most big churches have to buy property outside of where the population lives, sometimes anticipating where the city is moving towards. Then they pray, work and strategize to make their building and its ministries a big enough magnet to attract people. Many succeed at that, and I'm thrilled that they do.

But Small Churches are ideally suited to meet around a fountain in a mall if they do two things: keep a big vision, and stay on offense. They can also meet in a bar or a restaurant in the mall – and no, I don't mean buy the bar and transform it into a church building, I mean meet in the bar as people are drinking and talk about Christ's love to the people who are already there. I am most definitely not talking about some preacher hijacking the karaoke stage with his worship band and asking the bar patrons to sing along to "Shout to the Lord". That's institutional church thinking. Small Churches don't have to do it the institutional way.

Catching a Bigger Vision

So with all these possibilities at our fingertips, where are all the dynamic, big-vision Small Churches?

They're everywhere.

And there are more popping up every day.

For example, Frank Wooden is the pastor of 100-member Hope Church in San Diego California. In the past year they've planted three new churches, including a Spanish language congregation and two in the urban heart of San Diego. There are plans in place (not just hopes and dreams, but concrete *plans*) to launch several more campuses next year, eventually planting 50 neighborhood churches in Greater San Diego over the next decade.

I'll let Frank tell you why. "The philosophy behind the neighborhood approach is that each campus will have certain essentials in common with all the other campuses while maintaining distinctives that enable it to reach its neighborhood. The preaching at each campus will be live, not video, and many will be in Spanish. Fifty neighborhood campuses of 100-200 people will have a greater impact on a city like San Diego than one church of 5,000 in one location. This approach actually leverages smaller size as an advantage, rather than a disadvantage."

If I could replay my 20-year-old conversation with the pastor who was worried that none of the churches in my community were "doing anything," I'd gladly point him to churches of all sizes that are doing great things. They were then and they are now. I was just too blinded by The Grasshopper Myth to see them.

Yes, Small Churches with big vision are everywhere. But there aren't nearly enough of us. More New Small Churches need to be planted, and existing Small Churches need to become New Small Churches by discovering and embracing their own God-given bigger vision.

Chapter 9
An Open Letter

To My Fellow Small Church Pastors,

You and I have an awesome responsibility.

God has entrusted into our care the most powerful force on earth –
the Small Church.

That may not feel true for you right now. It may never have felt true
for you. Nevertheless it is true.

Let me prove it to you.

There are millions of us around the world. No matter how you tally
the numbers, by even the most conservative estimates, more people
have voluntarily placed their spiritual lives under our care than
under the care of any other group of people on earth.

Look at the raw numbers with me. By all accounts there are two
to three billion people who call themselves Christians and attend a
church on a regular basis. Let's go with the lowest of those numbers
– two billion people.

Of those two billion-plus people, <u>well over half of them voluntarily attend a local congregation of less than 350 people.</u>

<u>That's over one billion people</u> who choose to come to our churches.

If those numbers are true (and I assure you they are conservative), why do so many of us feel alone, frustrated, underachieving, even bitter instead of excited, empowered, vital and needed? And why is it likely that this is the first time in your life you've heard these facts about Small Church ministry?

Part of the reason is because this is probably the first book you have read on the subject of pastoring that wasn't written by a megachurch pastor or by a researcher whose main focus has been megachurches. That's not necessarily a bad thing, it's just the way it is.

I know your frustrations because I am one of you. For over 25 years I have been a Small Church pastor. 20 years and counting at the church I currently serve. My congregation has been as small as 35 and as large as 350. Currently it's just over 200.

Another reason Small Church pastors feel frustrated is that we've been told for years that a successful church is always a numerically growing church. That, conversely, only numerically growing churches are considered successful. Many of us have believed it. I know I have.

Yet a further reason for our frustration is that when we look deep into our hearts, as hard as we work, as passionate as we feel or have felt about ministry, most of us know we can do better than we've done.

But it's hard to do better when resources are limited, when difficult financial times hit people's voluntary donations first, when most of us have to work another non-ministry job full-time just to pay our family's (and the church's) bills, and when we feel like nobody cares about any of that, including denominational representatives, ministerial conference organizers, church growth advocates, pastoral book authors and, maybe most of all, other Small Church pastors. Why aren't we at least there for each other?

It's time for that to change.

Here are some more numbers. There are approximately 4,000 megachurches in the world providing the primary spiritual support for about 100 million people every week.

I stand in grateful awe of such ministry. Megachurch pastors have done, and continue to do a work for the kingdom of God that communities, cultures and nations should recognize and celebrate far more than they do.

Small Church pastors sometimes complain that megachurch pastors receive more credit than we do, but they also take an awful lot more heat than we do. On the weekend the Ted Haggard scandal broke, our church's youth group happened to be hosting a youth drama team from his Colorado Springs church. That Sunday morning God gave us the sad privilege of mourning with those kids while national attention was focused like a laser on their pastor and his sins. We need to remember that the megachurch spotlight that we sometimes wish was focused on our successes goes destructively supernova on our failures and sins.

Megachurch pastors are often the church's only face to much of the world. As fellow pastors we need to stand alongside them in our prayers. I personally want to say a huge "thank you" to those whose ministries I have personally benefited from, mostly through their books.

But, fellow Small Church pastors, the size of their task pales next to ours.

Again, run the numbers. Megachurch pastors oversee churches with weekly attendance figures of 2,000 to 20,000 to the largest congregation on earth with almost [gasp!] 1,000,000 congregants every week (Yoido Assembly of God in Seoul, South Korea). But it's still about 100 million people in megachurches at the most, while Small Church pastors are responsible for one billion people at the least.

Did you get that? Small Churches minister to 10 times more people every week than megachurches do! *Over one billion people!* That's more than any entire Christian denomination, including Catholics. More than all the Jews, Muslims, Hindus or Buddhists on earth.

Precisely because they are scattered in small groups across the face of the earth instead of being clumped together in larger quantities, Small Churches have immediate access to communities, families and individuals, making them the largest, most readily deployable force for spiritual transformation, emotional encouragement and material sustenance that the world has ever seen. It's time to turn them loose! Small Church pastors, our fingers are on the trigger. We can withhold or release this redemptive power on a world that has never needed us more than it needs us now.

This is an awesome and sacred responsibility.

I fear we have not met that responsibility well.

We need to do better. We can do better. With God's help we will do better.

No more feeling guilty that my church attendance isn't growing. No more working outside my primary gifting to do things that I and my church were never called to do. No more feeling jealous of the church down the street or trying to come up with some theological justification to despise the preacher on TV.

Instead, let's embrace who we are. Let's do what God is calling us to do. Let's pastor the church we've got, not the one we wish we had. When we do that, let the world stand and watch in amazement at what an army of Small Churches and the more than one billion people in them can do to bring the healing power of Christ to a hurting world.

Chapter 10
God Doesn't Take Attendance

Sitting in church is not the end game.

It never has been.

It's supposed to be a means to an end.

No matter what size their church is, every pastor faces the challenge of trying to walk people through the stages of spiritual growth. Specifically, it's hard to get some people past the stage where they believe that riding the pew for an hour or so in a weekend worship service fulfills some religious obligation in a heavenly attendance book.

Weekend services are supposed to be a time to worship, learn and fellowship so we can take that experience and live for Christ every day. If all we do is sit and endure, (or even sit and enjoy), we've missed the point. After all, as I like to remind my congregation, God doesn't take attendance.

Where do people get this mistaken idea about the primacy of church attendance? They get it from us, fellow pastors, they get it from us.

We tell our congregations in sermons, slogans, mission statements and baseball diamond graphics that church attendance isn't the end game. Then, in most of our subliminal communication, we give them the opposite message.

We tell them church attendance is what matters most to God...
...when we use attendance figures to determine a church's success or failure
...when we make it a sacrament
...when we set people up as an example of holiness because they're at church "every time the doors are open"
...when we give awards to churches whose weekend worship attendance has grown, while we ignore, try to fix, or try to close those that haven't
...when we spend massive amounts of time, money and work hours on attendance drives so we can brag, "there were _____ people in church last weekend!"
...when our spouses and children don't know whether to dread or to look forward to Sunday lunch with us until they see how full or empty the church is on Sunday morning
...when we criticize church families for spending too many weekends at the lake
...when we won't spend any weekends with our own family at the lake
...when we know how many people sat in our church today, but have no idea how many people are sleeping on the streets of our city tonight.

What Does God Count?

I know what some of you were thinking the moment you read the heading for this chapter. After all, I've read all the books and attended all the seminars you have.

"Of course God takes attendance!"

"What about souls?!"

"We count people because people count!"

"If God wasn't concerned with numbers there wouldn't be an entire book of the Bible called Numbers!"

That last one is my particular favorite. Yes, it's true that one of the sixty-six books of the Bible is called Numbers. It's also true that forty books of the Bible are named for individuals, including all four Gospels. Thirteen books are named after groups of people, and eight of those are named after towns, or regions, where people worshipped almost exclusively in house (therefore, *very* small) churches.

If you're keeping track, here's the score so far:

Bible, 66 books
Individuals, 40 books
People Groups, 13 books
Small Churches, 8 books
Numbers, 1 book

I'm perfectly willing to use the books-of-the-Bible scale to tell us how important numbers should be to us. Let's just be sure to use the *entire Bible* when we do so.

Before we move on from this topic, let's not pretend that most of us don't know the source of the "book of Numbers" or the "people count" quotes. The "people count" quote was made famous by Rick Warren in *The Purpose Driven Church* and it, along with the "book of Numbers" quote has been repeated by him in seminars so often that he's probably tired of hearing himself say them. I have some sympathy for where I think they come from.

I first heard Rick use those quotes when I attended one of his pastors' conferences back when most of Saddleback's church buildings were no more than glorified tents. It was a wonderfully helpful seminar from which I gained a lot of knowledge and sensed a huge amount of support from Rick's strong heart for fellow pastors.

At that time, much of the massive and mostly unwarranted criticism that was being leveled at him and other megachurch pastors was coming from people who believed that megachurches were a blight upon the kingdom of God merely because they were so big. That is as wrong-headed and mean-spirited as those who despise Small Churches for being small.

Rick Warren was put in the unfair position of having to defend his numerical success. I think the bulk of the criticism had more to do with jealousy than anything. And I have to admit, being geographically close enough to Saddleback that many people drive past my church to get to Rick's church every weekend, I've felt some of that jealousy myself.

All such jealousy is wrong. No, not just wrong. It is sin.

Many megachurch pastors have been a blessing to me and to millions of others. There's room in God's plan for all of us. Rick Warren should never have been forced to scramble for justification to excuse the fact that more people show up at his church than mine.

A couple years ago I had an "aha" moment that gave me some new and surprising insight into the phenomenon of why some pastors are inspired by numbers and others aren't. It was my first Catalyst conference in 2009. Andy Stanley was interviewing Rick Warren. (Conferences like this are another important ministry megachurches can provide that Small Churches cannot). The interview was light-hearted and the banter between these megachurch pastors seemed genuinely warm and friendly. At one point Andy asked Rick to address some of his critics, particularly those who say that megachurches are too numbers-oriented. Rick spoke passionately about it and he included his "book of Numbers" and "people count" quotes in his answer.

Later in the interview the subject switched to pastoral burnout. Warren wisely suggested that pastors need to honor the weekly Sabbath by devoting an entire day other than Sunday to doing things that aren't work-related. He said that since we work inside our own heads during the rest of the week it's a good idea to work with our hands on our Sabbath. Rick does that in his backyard garden, he told us. He loves the therapy of getting his hands in the dirt. I won't get the numbers right on this, but Rick got almost gleeful when he started telling Andy that he was currently growing twelve varieties of flowers, seven kinds of vegetables, nine types of fruit, and so on. Andy interrupted this listing to light-heartedly make the observation (and this *is* a direct quote), "Wow, Rick. You don't just count *people*, you count *everything*!" Big laughs ensued. From the audience and Rick.

There you go, I thought.

I do not doubt Rick Warren's passion for people. More people are brought to Christ and are legitimately discipled in any single year through the impact of his ministry than are likely to be saved and discipled through the entire lifetime of my ministry. I really believe that Rick Warren and many other megachurch pastors count people because people truly do count to them.

I also know this: *Some pastors count people because some pastors count everything!* That's who they are. They're numbers-oriented. That's how God made them and it's one of the ways they get and stay motivated. As Rick himself would say in his 301 C.L.A.S.S. discipleship curriculum, that's their heart.

But not all pastors are built that way. Most of us aren't. I know I'm not.

I'd rather live with people and tell their individual stories than recite numbers. I'd rather get to know people in a home group than work on the logistics of a city-wide campaign. I'd rather attend a megachurch conference than host one. And I'd rather see small-, medium, big, and megachurches link arms in a common quest than keep fighting about which size of church is the "right" size of church.

Love Counts

Why are we obsessed with church size? Is it because most pastors are men, and size comparison is what men do? Or have we just strayed that far from Jesus' original goal?

Love God. Love others. That's all.

Jesus told us that, loud and clear.

A few years ago I attended the memorial service of Mark Armstrong, a friend who pastored a Small Church in downtown Orange, California, near a spot called the Orange Circle. At the time of Mark's memorial I was keeping a daily journal for a college class assignment. This is what I wrote on the day of Mark's funeral:

> *I attended a memorial service today for a friend who had been a pastor of a very small church in the Orange Circle for 52 years. Less than 50 people most Sundays. To a lot of people, Mark's ministry probably seemed like the glory days had passed decades ago. I have to admit it seemed that way to me. But I liked him and enjoyed the encouragement he gave me when I'd drop by occasionally.*
>
> *What I didn't realize – and maybe nobody did until the funeral – was that my experience with him was multiplied among hundreds, maybe thousands of people until the day he died. The sanctuary, the fellowship hall and the outdoor lawn around his church building were packed with over 1,000 people today – including at least 50 pastors, some of whom talked about how Mark had reached out to them when they were down and had saved their ministry at a critical time.*
>
> *Here was a man who, almost invisibly, touched lives of common people around the Orange Circle, and of ministers and ministries around the world. We got a*

small glimpse of it today in a two-hour memorial service that could have gone for two days had everyone who wanted to say something been allowed to.

Love God, love others. Too often it's more of a slogan for me than a lifestyle. It wasn't a slogan to Mark. He lived it.

Until today I saw his life as average – maybe less than average. Today I saw it as the towering achievement it was. But unlike most comparisons of my life to a life of greatness, this one didn't intimidate me or make me feel inadequate. Mark didn't have extraordinary abilities. His success wasn't about what he did, but about who he was – and how much he loved.

Loving God and loving others is not a church growth strategy. It's not a means to an end. It is the means *and* the end. thats it !

It's not, "love God and love others, then your church seats will be filled," a sentiment I've heard at many pastoral seminars, by the way, though we wouldn't dare use those exact words. *We* say things like that, but Jesus never did.

Love God, love others, that's all. It was good enough for Jesus. Because it was good enough for Jesus it was good enough for my friend Mark. It should be good enough for the rest of us too.

The reason we're supposed to love God and love others isn't so that when we get to heaven we can hear Jesus say, "Well done, good and faithful servant, that strategy sure packed 'em in for the Christmas pageant!" We're supposed to love God and love others because (*get ready for it...*) God wants us to *actually love God and actually love others!* What a concept!

When we get to heaven I think the greatest thing we can hope to hear from the lips of Jesus will be, "Well done, my child, you loved

God and loved others. Now you get to spend eternity loving God and loving others."

In some settings, loving God and loving others will have the side result of attracting thousands of people into a Mega Cathedral. But that will not be the case in most settings. And that's OK.

The reason both mega and Small Churches sometimes have to fight to justify their size is as old as human nature. The Apostle Paul discovered this in the town of Corinth where they were constantly pitting one kind of Christian against another. His stern rebuke to them, capped by the sharp sting of sarcasm in the last verse, was as follows:

> In the following directives I have no praise for you, for your meetings do more harm than good. In the first place, I hear that when you come together as a church, there are divisions among you, and to some extent I believe it. No doubt there have to be differences among you to show which of you have God's approval. – 1 Corinthians 11:17-19

"There have to be *differences* among you to show which of you have God's *approval*." God couldn't possibly approve of small *and* megachurches, could he? Either Small Churches have to be failures at growing the kingdom and reaching people, or megachurches have to be heartless, soulless, people-pleasing, money-grubbing, religious entertainment complexes. They can't both be OK, can they?

People count. Whether it's two or three people who have come together in Jesus' name, or a crowd of 5,000-plus hungry souls, Jesus knew that each group is made up of individuals who are known personally by their creator. And for some reason he cares enough to have counted the hairs on each of their heads (a task that is easier to do on my head with every passing year).

Not to mention, the church is a family, according to the New Testament. How many families do you know that show their love for each other by counting their members every day? And how many people would say that a family with ten kids is more healthy or loving than a family, like mine, with three kids? Of course we wouldn't.

What makes a family healthy and loving has nothing to do with numbers. It should be the same in the family of God.

The Church God Wants to Grow

"Pastors and laypersons alike want their church to grow. And ... so does God!" Statements like that are often made without any serious challenge to the pre-suppositions behind them.

Yes, pastors want their churches to grow – I see it all the time. Sometimes we want it too much, and the price for such overwhelming desire can be very high.

But do laypeople want their church to grow? Does God?

More specifically, does God want *my* church to grow? Or does God want *the* church to grow?

I know I'm challenging conventional wisdom here, but doesn't conventional wisdom *need* to be challenged? And often?

One of the main complaints about Small Churches is that the only reason they stay small is because they have a small vision. I used to believe that. I don't anymore.

I was told that if my church wasn't growing numerically something was broken. That people who pastor or attend Small Churches were settling for less than God's best. That they had limited vision and passion. That they selfishly wanted to keep the gift of the Gospel to themselves. I didn't want that to be true of me or my church, so I nearly burnt myself out trying to solve those supposed problems.

As it turns out, my church wasn't broken until I tried to fix it.

When we minister to the people we've got and to the community around us we aren't settling or selfish. Once I discovered the New Small Church, I started to understand that its vision – and God's vision for it – happens to be HUGE.

Here's how big the vision of the New Small Church is. We are a unique, indispensable part of the work God is doing throughout the entire world. That work is too big to fit inside any building or denomination. It is too big for us to do alone. It is too big for me to grasp, to plan or to stop. It began with Jesus, is sustained by Jesus and won't be finished until Jesus says it's finished when he comes back again.

I don't know of any bigger vision than that.

When we concentrate so much of our efforts on growing individual church bodies, are we missing out on the bigger picture – and a bigger vision? Could it be that we have been limiting God's vision for *his* church by concentrating so much time, energy and money on trying to grow *my* church?

After all, Jesus never commanded us to build the church. He very clearly kept that job for himself when he said, "I will build my church..." And the growth of Jesus' church, thankfully, is not limited to the growth of the congregation I happen to be pastoring at any given time. Not only that, but since Jesus is in charge of growing *his* church, if we're doing the building by our efforts, our ideas and our charisma, maybe we should stop calling it a church at all.

Only Jesus builds churches.

So I wonder, could it be that obsessing over the growth of my church is actually a *smaller* vision than what Jesus had in mind? Is it possible that embracing God's vision for the entire Church, and accepting my much-needed role pastoring a Small Church within it, may actually be a *bigger* vision?

Maximum ≠ Optimum

Bigger isn't always better.

When pastors ask each other if our churches are growing, the question we're always — and I mean *always* — asking is *are we getting bigger*?

Every year our church fills out a report on the vital statistics of the congregation — weekend attendance, tithing, missions giving, salvations, baptisms, etc. I understand the need for record-keeping. I also know that if the only thing you knew about our church was what you read in that report, we'd look like we were plateaued at best, and shrinking at worst. Our Sunday attendance has been fairly level for a few years now, and the current worldwide financial challenges have dropped our offerings by about one-third from their peak.

My church isn't getting bigger. Not by Sunday morning attendance numbers. Statistically, we're one of those sad, under-achieving plateaued churches that cause denominational officials and church analysts to call emergency meetings to figure out how to fix us.

But we don't need fixing, because we *are* growing. We have been for years now. The people in our church are happy and excited to get together, they're proud to bring their friends and family members with them. The building is in use six days every week and seven days most weeks, from about six am to after nine pm. Not for committee meetings (we have very few of those), but for actual ministry.

The homes of our church members are active with small groups and our Intern House is filled with young people who commit a year or two of their lives to move in and work with us. Marriages are being mended. The homeless are being loved and fed. A church in Mexico greets us with big smiles when we visit several times a year with hope and material goods. Every day of the year dozens of church members work to raise money so they can spend their vacation week on a missions trip to Panama, Zimbabwe, Northern Ireland et al, instead of lounging on the beach. And I haven't scratched the surface of what happens in our preschool, daycare, summer camps, retreats and more.

Sometimes what we call a plateau is simply a church reaching its optimal size, then using that size to grow healthful fruit.

One of the worst things a church can do, once it has reached optimum, is to keep pushing for maximum.

But we do that. I did that.

I wanted the church to be better – I still want that – and I was convinced that better meant bigger.

I was wrong.

No church has unlimited resources. Yes, we have a limitless God. But I'm not him. I have limits, and so does my church. It's not healthy, godly or helpful to push a church to places God isn't asking it to go in order to meet some artificial numerical standard or stroke the pastor's ego. Even if we call it faith.

If a church's optimal size is 150-200, is it fair to say they've shrunk if their average attendance drops from 180 to 170 for a while? Have they plateaued if they've shifted major portions of their energies into a successful weeknight recovery ministry or outside-the-walls ministry to the poor, but haven't added butts in the seats on Sunday?

There are many ways to grow, even if your building, your calling, your gifts or your congregational style means you'll always run Sunday morning numbers that others consider low. The challenge, once that size is reached, is to figure out what growth looks like now.

Can a church be too small and not reaching its potential? Yes. We see examples of it every day, with church buildings sitting empty all week (and mostly empty on weekends too) and having little or no impact on their community.

Can a church be too big, as well as too small? I say yes to that too. Ill-health in a big church is less obvious, but some megachurches are little more than vanity projects for the pastor, status clubs for the wealthy or places that provide a false sense of spiritual security for people who think God takes attendance.

Not all growth is numerical. If you're in a church that's healthy, where people are growing in their faith, reaching the community, investing in missions and seeing transformed lives and families, it's shameful, even sinful, to divert our limited attention, money, time, energy and heart away from that into chasing numbers.

We don't pressure congregation members to reach a "soul quota" of people they must lead to faith in Jesus – at least we shouldn't do that. Pastors, we should stop pressuring ourselves and our fellow pastors to do it too. One person may be called by God to participate in reaching thousands of people for Christ, while another believer satisfies the call of God on her life by caring for an aging relative for 20 years so they can pass into the arms of Jesus knowing they were loved by him because they were loved by their family while their frail body was here among us.

Every person and every church has their calling and its corresponding joys and burdens.

Chapter 11

A New Way to Define Success

"In the United States, numbers impress us. ...We measure churches by how many members they boast. ... Jesus questioned the authenticity of this kind of record-keeping."
– Francis Chan

The one word in the above quote that immediately jumps out at me is "boast". I don't think Francis Chan chose it by mistake. I think he's seen and heard a lot of the same conversations and pastoral reports that I have.

At yet another ministerial conference, one of the speakers told us about conversations he used to have with another pastor. When they were ministering at churches in different parts of the country they'd catch up occasionally over the phone. The second pastor's church was growing at an alarmingly fast rate, and is a well-known megachurch today. The first pastor, who was telling us this story, was having only modest growth at a church of just a few hundred.

The reason for sharing these conversations with us, he said, was to tell us how important it is to encourage each other in the ministry – a laudable goal. He told us how this megachurch pastor encouraged him, especially when he was feeling bad that his church wasn't growing at anywhere near the same rapid pace. "He'd always tell me 'hey, that's great! At that size, your church is in the top 15% percent of the churches in the country', then 12%, then 10% and so on."

Is it just me or does it concern anyone else that the best way one pastor can think of to encourage another pastor is to put down the other 85% of churches and pastors in the country, then 88%, then 90% and so on? I know that wasn't his intent, but that's the implication. *You're better than those other pastors and churches* is what he was saying.

Is that appropriate encouragement? Or does it reinforce a wrong way of assessing the value of a church? Wouldn't it be better if, instead of trading attendance figures, when pastors got together we'd share stories of life transformation and healing? Obviously there was ministry happening in the first pastor's smaller church. It should stand on its own as a testimony of God's grace without the need to compare his church with anyone else's.

Instead we boast. We're so used to boasting that, even when we're trying to lift up another pastor we boast about their church as compared to others.

What Does a Healthy Church Produce?

If we pay less attention to counting butts in the seats, how do we measure success?

Shortly after having my heart changed about the value of church size, I put that question to the volunteer leaders of our church at our annual vision-casting weekend. The answer was obvious to them. I think they were shocked that I asked it – and maybe disappointed in their fearless leader for not knowing the answer myself.

"I think we should measure success the way Jesus did," was the immediate and overwhelming response. "One person at a time.

Are individual people growing? Is the community being impacted? That's what matters."

More and more people are agreeing with this, and saying so out loud. In *UNChristian*, David Kinnaman, president of the Barna Institute, has found that many believers and non-believers alike are saying, "We should measure success not merely by the size of our church ... but also by the depth and quality of spiritual growth in people's lives."

Helmut Thielicke was a German theologian whose writings are usually even more intimidating than his name. But he wrote a very accessible book entitled *A Little Exercise for Young Theologians*. The premise was that as trained, professional ministers we need to be careful not to think we have all the answers. There's a pool of readily accessible wisdom that we often overlook – the people seated in front of us every weekend.

Thielicke encouraged his readers not to go chasing after every new theological idea or ministerial strategy, but to test it all against scripture and to measure it against "the spiritual instinct of the children of God."

That stuffy old German was right. So were my wonderful, faithful, wise and patient church leaders. We need to measure success the way Jesus did. One person at a time.

In an earlier chapter we talked about the problems of one type of church despising the other. But there may be no more frequent place where this unchristian despising takes place than from clergy to laity (an unhealthy and unbiblical pair of terms we need to start banishing from our lexicon). Nowhere does this despising flow more readily than on the subject of church growth.

As also referred to earlier, we're actually set up for this despising of laity by clergy at church growth conferences when we're told that anyone at the church who opposes the wonderful new ideas we're learning are the sticks-in-the-mud and vision-killers.

Again, Thielicke speaks to this. When we, as ministers, are excited about a new idea, he suggests that if the idea "does not take more seriously the objections of the ordinary washerwoman and the simple hourly wage earner ... surely something is not right with the theology. If, in short, the so-called ordinary congregation is somewhat skeptical about theology, this skepticism is by no means naïve."

If the people don't like it we should listen to them. They are the church, after all.

Malcolm Gladwell also referred to this phenomenon, although not in church circles, in his groundbreaking book *Blink*. The premise of the book is that sometimes a fresh new set of eyes can see in a moment (a *blink*) a truth that the world's great experts are clouded on because they've been too close to it with all their detailed study. The big picture can get lost in the details and the advanced learning can get in the way of common sense. The non-expert (or an expert with fresh eyes) may not even know how to say what's wrong, they just *feel* it.

When we despise those feelings, those nudges, we do so at our, and the church's, peril. Sometimes those nudges are the prompting of the Holy Spirit.

So, back to the advice of my church volunteer leaders. Counting success one person at a time. Individual growth. Do we even know what that looks like? Yes we do. But it's like art. We know it when we see it, but we have no way of quantifying it. That's where our discomfort comes from.

We want numbers to verify our successes.

There are two huge problems with that sentence – and they're found in the words "numbers" and "our". First, not all successes have *numbers* to verify them. Second, the successes of the church are not *our* successes. We need to start getting comfortable, in the first instance, with Success Without Numbers and in the second instance, with Success That's Not Ours.

Success Without Numbers

For years I was told and believed another premise of the church growth movement. That, just like the fruit of a healthy tree is other trees, the fruit of a healthy church is other churches. I believed it because it's the truth. Unfortunately it's not the *whole* truth.

Half the fruit of a healthy tree is another tree. The other half of the fruit of a healthy tree is, not surprisingly, *fruit*. Not all seeds are destined for the numerical growth of other trees. Most aren't. Most seeds get eaten with the fruit while it's offering its life-sustaining energy for the benefit of others. It gets consumed, not planted. Sorry, all my seed-faith friends, you do need to eat some of your seed.

It's easy to calculate the value of healthy seeds that plant other trees because you can count those new trees. It's much harder to calculate the value of the healthful fruit that is eaten by the farmer's family. But that use of fruit is just as valuable. It could even be argued that the eating of healthful fruit is the ultimate goal of the seed, rather than the planting of other healthy trees. After all, if all the seeds are being planted but none of the fruit is being eaten, what are we planting the trees for?

Both uses of the fruit and seeds are valuable. But, unlike the tree-producing-a-tree-metaphor, the tree-producing-fruit metaphor *is* in the Bible. Jesus never said anything about trees needing to produce other trees. What he did say was, "Every tree that does not bear good *fruit* is cut down and thrown into the fire. Thus, by their *fruit* you will recognize them." Also, when Jesus cursed the fig tree, he didn't do so because he wanted to get seeds from it to plant other trees. He got angry because he was hungry and it was offering him nothing to eat.

Not every church is called to formally plant other churches. Their main job is to feed the flock – just like Jesus told Peter to do. That is success. And it is truly *immeasurable* – in both senses of that word.

Success That's Not Ours

There's an old saying that goes, "there's no limit to what a person can do if they don't care who gets the credit."

Close, but not quite true.

Certainly it would be great if we could all remove our egos from the equation, which is what the quote is all about. But more accurately, and more biblically, there is one way in which it matters who gets the credit. We need to be sure all the credit goes to Jesus.

One more time I refer you to the most important church growth verse in the Bible. Jesus said, "I will build my church." Again, there are two key words in that quote. "I" and "my".

As we've already talked about, these two words tell us it's Christ's church, not ours, so he gets the credit for building it.

When Jesus gets the credit, I should be just as thrilled when my efforts put someone into a healthy church down the street or around the world as I am when they come to the church I'm pastoring. That's what a lot of Small Churches have as their mission. They're senders, not attracters. They may not be growing numerically in their church building and may never formally plant another church body, but the people who are eating of their fruit are growing personally and dropping seeds everywhere they go.

Again, that doesn't give us numbers for our annual church reports, so no one may see the results of that work except God. But God does. That should be enough.

When each of my children got old enough to start working, I gave all three the same advice as they went nervously to their first day on the job. I told them to approach every day with three rules in mind. First, show up ready to work on time or early. Second, give it all you've got when you're there. Third, don't take anything that's not yours when you leave. If you do that, I told them, you'll always be a desirable employee.

Those are good rules to apply to pastoring. First, let's show up ready to go, physically, emotionally, mentally and spiritually for the job we've got, instead of dreaming about the job we wish we had. Second, let's apply everything we've got to doing the best we can, then with God's help, better things will happen than we're actually capable of. Third, at the end of the day, don't take anything that doesn't belong to us. Leave all the blame in the garbage can, and give all the glory to God.

Jesus and Crowds – An Unhappy Marriage

Many church growth books devote significant ink to telling their readers how Jesus attracted crowds. What many of them don't say is that, while Jesus' ministry did attract crowds – megachurch-sized crowds at times – he actually spent more time trying to *avoid* crowds than trying to *draw* them.

Not only that, but many of the methods they say Jesus employed to attract crowds were actually used to thin them out. His parables for instance. How many church growth strategists have told me that I need to tell more stories because that's one of the ways Jesus grew a crowd?

That's not what the Bible says. Yes, Jesus told parables. Lots of them. But he was also very clear that the reason he told them wasn't to *attract* crowds, but to *reduce* them. As Jesus told his disciples, "The knowledge of the secrets of the kingdom of God has been given to you, but to others I speak in parables, so that, 'though seeing, they may not see; though hearing, they may not understand.'" (Luke 8:10)

Recently at Cornerstone we completed a ten-week Sunday morning series through the life of Christ. The idea was to focus less on the details and more on the big-picture themes of Christ's life and ministry. One of the things we noticed in this approach was that when Jesus attracted crowds it was almost always unintentional and unwanted.

Instead of hiring a marketing team, Jesus often used tactics (including parables) to intentionally *shrink* the size of the crowds. For instance, the reason Jesus had to perform a miracle to feed the 5,000 was because they were in a "remote place" where Jesus had gone to escape the crowds. The people were there because they had heard where he was going and "ran on foot from all the towns and got there ahead of them." Later, when he was talking to the father whose son was demon-possessed, Jesus abruptly stopped the conversation and healed the boy to *avoid* a crowd that was beginning to gather.

Here's how extreme Jesus' aversion to crowds was. When Jesus started talking in earnest about the necessity of his impending death, the crowd, including many disciples, couldn't handle the truth of it. Instead of moderating his language in order not to offend people, Jesus pushed them further. He added that, not only was it important to accept the cross, but:

> Jesus said to them, "I tell you the truth, unless you eat the flesh of the Son of Man and drink his blood, you have no life in you. Whoever eats my flesh and drinks my blood has eternal life, and I will raise him up at the last day. For my flesh is real food and my blood is real drink. Whoever eats my flesh and drinks my blood remains in me, and I in him. Just as the living Father sent me and I live because of the Father, so the one who feeds on me will live because of me. ... On hearing it, many of his disciples said, "This is a hard teaching. Who can accept it?" Aware that his disciples were grumbling about this, Jesus said to them, "Does this offend you?" (John 6:53-57, 60-62)

"Does this offend you?" Jesus asked them. Of course it offended them. It was *intended* to offend them! Jesus told them about his death in a way that made it appear as if he was promoting cannibalism as a necessary part of being his follower – *cannibalism*!

When the disciples tried to help him out by letting him know how repulsive this teaching was, Jesus did nothing to correct any possible misunderstandings. Instead, he let the thought of possible cannibalism hang in the air until, not surprisingly, "From this time many of his disciples turned back and no longer followed him." Then, instead of chasing after those who were leaving, Jesus turned to the Twelve and opened the back door for them by asking, "You do not want to leave too, do you?"

That's not a recommended strategy in any church growth book I've ever read. It's not one I'd recommend either. As much as I admire the WWJD? sentiment, there are definitely things Jesus did that his followers should *never* attempt. Literally walking off the beach onto a stormy lake without a boat comes to mind.

Passages like this should be considered whenever we're tempted to make incorrect assumptions. Just because we want bigger and bigger crowds at our church, doesn't mean Jesus wants the same thing.

More Than Butts and Bucks

A few years ago, when our church started putting together ideas for a website, I ran into a web designer at a pastoral convention who offered to meet with us for free. Free is good, so I set up the meeting.

He arrived at our church building a few weeks later. I gave him the five-minute tour of the church building, and by the time we were seated in my office I could tell I was losing him. Meetings like this were designed to sell his web design and site maintenance services, and the facility he'd just seen told him this would not be as big an account as he'd hoped. He was one of the guys I mentioned a few chapters ago who asked where the sanctuary was as we were standing in it.

He started by asking us what our vision was for the church's website. I tried to lift his spirits by letting him know that we weren't intending on limiting the ministry of the church to the size of our building. Our website should be more than an electronic bulletin. Instead, we wanted to use the internet as one of many avenues to expand the ministry of the church. That seemed to encourage him, so he started his pitch.

Everything he showed us that day about how to build a successful church website was designed to do two things: put butts in the seats and bucks in the offering. After a while I interrupted his pitch. That's a part of what we want to do, I assured him. Having more people come on Sunday and increasing our financial resources is always helpful. But that wasn't the main goal.

"Here's my idea," I told him. "I want to use this website, not just to *promote* ministry, but to actually *do* ministry. I want to put Sunday messages, articles, prayer partners, addiction recovery guidelines, salvation counselors and a host of other things I haven't even thought of yet on the website so that people from Denver to Dublin can be ministered to by our church even if they never set foot in it or send a dollar to us.

"Our church building is small. Using a website just to get more people into this building is too small a vision because our building is too limited in how many people it can hold. Even if we built the biggest church building the world had ever seen it would be puny compared to the numbers of people we can reach on the internet. What can you do to help us get started on something like that?" (As a side note, if you go to our church website you will see that it has not reached those lofty goals – yet).

The web guru was stunned. He tried to convince us that this wasn't a viable approach by showing us what some of the bigger churches he'd worked with had done. About the only thing I remember was that they all had a "Giving" button featured prominently on every page. He kept coming back to how well that worked.

I don't really blame him for that thought process. I had it myself for several years, so I know where it comes from. He just couldn't conceive of the idea that someone might log on and hear a message from our church, perhaps give their life to Christ, then attend *someone else's church.* That was not what he considered a valid use of ministry resources and a legitimate way to conceive of church growth. If there was no chance of that person ever coming to our physical church building to be counted in the Sunday morning attendance figures, he had nothing that could help me. I actually sensed that he thought of me as naïve for thinking this way.

It's time for me to say something ministers aren't supposed to admit – not even to ourselves.

Do you want to know the main reasons pastors emphasize weekend worship attendance over all other measures of church growth or health?

That's when we receive the offering. It's about bucks.

That doesn't mean weekend services aren't vital to the life of the church, or that taking great care about who does and doesn't attend them isn't valid. In most churches, including mine, weekend worship remains the focal point from which all other ministries of the church flow – and rightly so. But the fact that this is when we receive the offering looms very high on the scale of importance for many church leaders. You mess with Sunday and you mess with payday. Nobody messes with payday.

The other reason weekend worship attendance has taken on such exaggerated importance is that, while we're not supposed to measure ourselves against each other, we do it in our churches all the time. It's about butts in the seats. Sometimes when I'm at ministerial conferences it feels like the T-ball game where we tell the kids that no one keeps score, but every adult knows which team has the most runs.

Could it be that Jesus is trying to tell us that he isn't concerned about bucks and butts? That he's actually concerned about people? Even people who will never sit in our church? If *he* is, maybe *we* should be too.

Identifying With People In Need

One of the reasons I admire Rick Warren, despite my obvious readiness to disagree with him sometimes, is his transparency. For instance, in *The Purpose Driven Church* he says he planted Saddleback Church in Lake Forest because of demographics. He wanted to go where the people were going and his research had shown him that south Orange County California was the #1 place for population growth at the time. It also happened to be where the population would be upwardly mobile and young.

But what about pastors who are called to towns where the population is leaving? Or aging? Or downwardly mobile? In many of these places, a church will never be big – at least not for a generation or two. Spending time and money to build a megachurch in a poverty-stricken area may not be the right thing to do. A grand, ornate building may send the wrong message to the community about the priorities of the church.

There are some situations in which a megachurch is impossible or inappropriate. But there is no place on earth where a Small Church won't fit. In some situations, features that are often perceived as the weaknesses of Small Churches may actually be a great advantage, especially when working among the disenfranchised and disadvantaged. For example, Small Churches have more familiarity with failure – and more sympathy with the failure of others.

Yes, you read that right. There is value in failure.

Some time ago I was watching a worship DVD filmed in a massive arena by world-class musicians with thousands of worshippers singing along. One of their songs was about moving from glory to glory. It was a joyous experience, but it struck me that *glory to glory* was fairly easy to sing in that setting. The same song would mean something very different in a Small Church in an impoverished town.

When a Small Church pastor with a Small Church salary (which often means no salary at all) leads an equally poor, struggling congregation in singing about moving from glory to glory, there's an amount of faith needed that only struggling people can share.

Megachurches are wonderful places to rejoice with those who rejoice. But I thank God for those brave Small Church pastors in poverty-stricken locations who give their lives to weep with those who weep.

The Church That's Needed at the Time

The world needs all kinds of churches. Big, small, house, multi-site, ethnic, cross-ethnic, Pentecostal, high liturgy, low liturgy, teaching centers, salvation stations, independent, denominational, online, traditional, non-traditional and new types no one has thought about yet.

Just as people with various spiritual gifts are needed in the body of Christ, churches with different gifts are needed too. Immediately after a thorough explanation of the gifts, and right before explaining the pre-eminence of love, the Apostle Paul tells us that we are to "eagerly desire the greater gifts." Since Paul appears to give no hierarchy of gifts, the greater or best gift is generally considered to be the one that's most needed at the time. Preaching is less valuable than giving when someone is hungry, while administration is of greater benefit than prophecy when the finances need to be properly accounted for.

Many people are staunch advocates that the church needs to do things the way the New Testament church did them. I've never been a big fan of that approach for four reasons.

First, not everything the New Testament church did was perfect.

Jesus was perfect, but the early apostles were not. They even disagreed about how to do church. That's what the Jerusalem Council was called for. And the decision they arrived at feels like a compromise to many biblical scholars.

Second, we don't know as much about the structure of the early church and its meetings as we'd like to, or as we think we do. Much of what we "know" is speculation, and that's never a good foundation.

For instance, there are those who "know" that the early church consisted only of house churches, and those who "know" with equal certainty that the church was founded on an instant megachurch. The instant megachurch idea comes, of course, from the Acts 2 narrative which tells us that on the day of Pentecost, the birthday of the church, there were 3,000 added to the church. Bam! Instant megachurch, right?

Not so fast.

At least sixteen nations, provinces and/or ethnic groups were represented in the Day of Pentecost crowd. Adding Jerusalem as a seventeenth group, that's an average of 180 people from each region. Presumably most of them went back to their homes within days.

Assuming there was a much larger representation from Jerusalem, the average number of people from those other regions drops even smaller, making it likely that many churches in those areas were made up of little more than the "two or three" Jesus referred to. And while it is possible, even likely, that Jerusalem started with a large church of over 1,000 people, we have no idea if they met in smaller groups, all in one place or in a combination of large and small groups. So it's quite possible that when the church met to worship around the world in the weeks following the Day of Pentecost, the percentage of mega, to big, to mid, to small, to house churches may not have been much different than it is today.

Acts 2 proves nothing about God's preferred size or style of church. I think he meant to leave the question open. Let's stop pretending we know things when we don't know them for certain at all.

Third, not everything the early church did was solely for theological reasons. Some of it was done out of cultural preference or circumstantial necessity. Sharing all things in common, for instance. While laudable, it wasn't a command so much as a necessity borne of persecution. It was how they protected each other and kept their possessions from seizure by the Romans. Ananias and Saphirra didn't end up dead at the hand of the Holy Spirit because they failed to give all their money from the sale of their house to the apostles, but because they lied about it. Peter specifically pled with Ananias, "Didn't it belong to you before it was sold? And after it was sold, wasn't the money at your disposal?"

Fourth, and finally, there wasn't just one New Testament church, there were many. When someone says "we need to do church the way the early church did it," we need to ask, "which church are you referring to?" The church in Philadelphia was very different from the one in Laeodecia, while the Jerusalem and Corinth churches might have had a hard time recognizing each other as Christian at all.

Most of the letters Paul wrote were to specific churches. John wrote the book of Revelation, not to "the church" in general but to seven individual congregations with seven different messages tailored to the size, health, histories, sins and ministries of each church.

While there were both small and large gatherings in the first century church, there is nothing the New Testament church did that could not be done today if we only had Small Churches. But there are several things that couldn't be done if all we had were megachurches. Some of the ways we connect with God, with each other and with the community can only happen when the group is small.

Living in a Flat World

In the past several years, fewer books have had an impact on the way politicians and businesspeople see the world than Thomas L. Friedman's *The World is Flat.* In it, Friedman convincingly makes the case that the world has changed from using a top-down, institutionalized model of delivering one-size-fits-all goods and services through large-scale industrial structures, into a sideways, network-based model in which a teen with a laptop anywhere on earth can start a world-wide craze by delivering real-time services that people anywhere can personalize to suit their own needs.

Such a flat world is the perfect breeding ground for the God-breathed work that can be done through a network of vibrant churches, whether they're small or mega. We don't need large buildings, top-down structures or huge amounts of money to get the job done.

Most big churches and many denominations were birthed within a modernist mindset of using a top-down, multi-layered delivery system for goods and services to large populations. In referring to this modernist mindset, John Eldredge wrote, "We take the latest marketing methods, the newest business management fad, and we apply it to ministry" with the end result that, by Eldredge's reckoning, "it removes any real conversation with God."

Today, we can market to ever-smaller niches of people without any top-down bureaucracy. It seems the world is ready, more than ever, to be impacted by the kingdom of God through Small Churches with little or no official denominational connections to each other, linked together to change the world.

It's also important to note that historically, the times of the church's strongest growth and purest faith were when Small Churches, linked through informal networks, dominated the landscape. There were few large congregations during the early church, the Pentecostal revival or in China or Latin America today. But their spiritual awakenings were, and are, huge.

Conversely, the times when the church was at its weakest spiritually and most corrupt morally and politically were when top-down structures, megachurches and strong denominationalism were dominant. The Crusades and the Televangelism scandals come most readily to mind.

It's not that one form is inherently more or less corruptible than any other. After all there have been Elmer Gantrys in Small Churches and there are plenty of healthy, humble big churches. But success, institutionalism and wealth, not failure and poverty, have always been and will always be the greatest corrupting influences on the body of Christ.

Blessed are the Geeks

Donald Miller has an off-beat way of looking at the world and faith in Jesus. One of the things that gives him his unique take on things is that, as he puts it, "I don't like institutionalized anything".

In his break-through, quirky book *Blue Like Jazz,* he explored some of his experiences with God and the church and came to the conclusion that he's not a fan of people who try to make Christianity cool because he believes "There is nothing relevant about Christian spirituality."

I agree.

"Cool" is way overrated.

I'd rather spend my time stuck in an elevator with geeks who know they're geeks than in the world's grandest, most luxurious venue surrounded by beautiful people trying to "out-cool" each other.

It's one of the reasons I, and many others, like Small Churches. Small Churches are seldom smooth, corporate, institutional or cool. That may be one of the coolest things about them.

Chapter 12

Stages In the Emotional Life of the Small Church Pastor

Dr. Elisabeth Kübler-Ross gave the world a great gift when she wrote *On Death and Dying* in the 1960s. Her book forever enhanced our understanding of what people go through when they suffer loss, especially the death of a loved one.

Every person who has ever said, "you're in denial" is referencing her work, even if they don't realize it. Denial is the first of her five stages, followed by anger, bargaining, depression and acceptance. Her outline of the phases of grief has led to many other studies that have helped us understand the stages people go through in many aspects of life.

I have become convinced that most Small Church pastors go through emotional stages too. At the end, they either burn out and leave the ministry, or they go through that wall to effectiveness and fulfillment in ministry.

The stages I will outline are not the result of a scientific study. They are based on watching and participating in the lives of other Small

Church pastors and on my own first-hand experiences. I offer them as a starting point for discussion, encouragement and a possible path to finding God's grace and healing.

Stage 1 – Idealism & Innocence

A young person graduates from seminary or a ministerial internship to embark on a life in full-time ministry. All is fresh and new in this "first love" stage. The world is a blank slate, fresh out of the box, filled with nothing but possibilities.

I love being around young ministers in this wide-eyed place of idealism and naiveté.

I swear they even have that new car smell.

The first-time pastor steps into his new role with all the faith and gusto he's supposed to have. Whether he's working with a core group to start a brand-new church with a trendy name, or stepping into an existing fellowship with a difficult history, he believes that even the toughest neighborhood can be reached, the strangest new idea can work, and the church with an aging, static population can become healthy and grow. He just needs to work hard, love the people, stick to the Bible and pray.

Armed with that idealism, life in full-time ministry begins.

Stage 2 – Trust & Excitement

A couple years pass, and after an initial honeymoon stage of promising growth, church attendance plateaus or declines for a while. Recently there have been a couple board meetings in which some members have behaved in a surprisingly un-Christ-like manner. A handful of his most dependable people have actually left the church, some expressing a vague complaint that they're "not being fed". Others have just drifted away without even saying goodbye.

The still-idealistic young Pastor starts realizing that more is needed to grow a healthy church than hard work and God's Word, so he turns to experts he trusts. He starts reading their books, attending conferences, perhaps seeking out a personal mentor.

He is assured that church growth is not only possible, but a virtual certainty if he adds these proven strategies to what he's already doing and uses others to correct some errors he's been making. He trusts what he's being told because he's seen the visible results in the churches of the pastors he's listening to.

The pastor gets excited all over again, this time about trying these methods in his own church.

Stage 3 – Frustration & Disillusionment

A few more years pass as he experiments with various church growth strategies. Most of them have something that seems to help, but none of the strategies do for his church what they have done for others. But he doesn't give up. He knows the Lord will lead him to the one strategy that will work for him and his church. He just needs to have faith and put that faith to wise use.

Congregation members want their church to grow and want to support their pastor, so they sign on emotionally and financially with the first strategy. When that fails, they still sign on for the second and even third strategies. Yet they start to grow frustrated before their pastor does. Some express their growing confusion with questions like, "Pastor, why do you keep going to those conferences and reading those books? Why don't we just do church the way the Bible says?" That sounds so naïve to the pastor now. He's more convinced than ever that growing a church requires a special *something* he just hasn't found yet.

Soon he admits to himself that there may be more going wrong than failing to identify the right strategy. *Maybe this isn't the church I'm supposed to be in after all*, he wonders. If these feelings persist he may become disheartened enough to resign and move to a new church. But the cycle just starts all over again in the new city.

Disillusionment sets in and he begins questioning if maybe there's something wrong on an even deeper level. This is the first time the not-so-young-and-fresh pastor considers that he may have misread God's will for his life entirely. Maybe he's not called into pastoral ministry after all.

He looks around and notices many of his peers succeeding in visible ways, both in and outside of full-time ministry. *That should be me*, he silently whines.

Stage 4 – Anger & Isolation

After the next few church members leave, the now jaded pastor gets angry. *Good riddance*, he tells himself, and almost tells them.

He still picks up the occasional church growth book and goes to the usual conferences, but now it's more out of habit than with any real expectation. He avoids the fellowship meetings he used to crave because he doesn't want to talk about the church. Then one day he finds himself lying to another pastor when he's asked how his church is doing. He tells his colleague that their church is succeeding at a ministry they haven't done for a year, and leads him to believe that the church is double the size it actually is. He just can't stand to see another look of pity or hear one more person offer an attempt at uplifting phrases like, "don't worry, God's in control. It'll turn around. I'll be praying for you."

When he hears stories of how other churches are growing, he's no longer encouraged or excited about how many people's lives are being touched by the Gospel anymore. He's jealous that it's not happening in his church. Other church's success stories cause his frustration, anger and depression to deepen.

At this point, he may try to reach out to a fellow pastor or denominational official. They listen with a sympathetic ear, promise to pray, and tell him to "call me if I can help". After that first meeting he never hears from them again.

Isolated, bitter and angry, the loneliness becomes toxic.

Stage 5 – Burnout & Resignation

Years of failed efforts are now taking their toll at church and at home. His prayer life is non-existent, finances are getting tighter, arguments with his wife have replaced their sex life, and he snaps at the kids more quickly than he used to. They haven't had a vacation in years. Motivated by guilt instead of passion for ministry, he won't even allow himself a weekend off.

Old temptations that he hadn't thought about for years start tugging on him. It's subtle at first. Nothing wrong with an extra beer or two to unwind or a quick look at a pretty girl online, he tells himself. It's a pressure-reliever, that's all.

With finances getting tough, he may use some of the church funds to cover this month's personal bills, knowing he'll put it back when he gets his next paycheck. It's just a payday advance, really. After he does it the first time, it's easier to do the next time. He dips into the church funds more frequently, changing a line or two in the church books to cover his tracks until he can make it up. These behaviors cause him to be secretive about everything he does, deepening his sense of isolation even further.

Soon he's sneaking out of the office to drink during the day, gambling at the track, or seeking an inappropriate relationship from an equally lonely, vulnerable woman who offers him more sympathy than his discouraged, busy wife. He even uses his position of perceived moral authority to tell her this is what God would want them to do.

If you think this is overly dramatic, unfortunately it's not. When

I was going through my own battle with anger and depression I called a counselor at a free ministerial helpline set up by our denomination. The first thing the phone counselor did was ask me a series of about 20 questions, including Are you drinking a lot? Watching pornography? Gambling? Doing drugs? Sleeping with other women? With other men? Have you stolen money from the church? etc.

When I truthfully answered "No" to all the questions, he asked, "Then why are you calling me?"

"Because I need help." I told him. "I'm an emotional wreck. I'm worried that if I don't get help soon, one of those could be my next step." He assured me I was going to be OK if I got the help I needed. When I asked him how he could be so sure of that, he told me I was the first pastor who had ever called him who hadn't answered "Yes" to at least one of those questions.

This is the stage when pastors often leave the ministry entirely. For one or more of several reasons. Some get caught in their sin by their church or their wife. Some just walk away and find non-church employment. Some get fired by the church for not doing their job well. Some run off with another woman – or man.

For those who stay in their church, many do so only because of financial necessity. They can't find another church to minister in and they don't have a secular skill. When that happens, the pastor and church often spend years just going through the motions. He resigns himself to a life of mediocrity. Inertia sets in and any real ministry just stops happening.

It's often at this point that others look at the Small Church with the pastor who has obviously given up and say things like, "isn't that typical. No wonder that church is small. He's not even trying."

But the reasons are never as simple as they seem.

Stage 6 – Redefinition & Contentment

With nothing to lose, and nowhere else to turn, the pastor can reverse this trend if he finally does the two things necessary to get out of this downward cycle. Be honest, with himself and those who love him, and ask for help.

If he's made it through the previous stage without causing too much damage to himself and others, his emotional and spiritual health, along with his ministry, can be restored within two to three years. If the sin and its subsequent damage have been severe, restoration will take much longer and it will not come without significant loss and pain. In severe situations, full-time ministry may never happen again.

The pastor who has not fallen into deep sin and is finally willing to seek consistent, biblically-based help through a counselor or mentor can usually start the turn-around very quickly. It always involves a redefinition of what it means to be successful in ministry. Those old concepts are hard to let go of, but when he does release them he finally sees them for the burden they were.

Then, not surprisingly, he finds that his *new* definition of success in ministry is pretty close to a *very old* definition of success in ministry.

He learns to stop worrying about how many empty seats there are and starts loving the people who are there, and not just because it's in his job description. He becomes truly grateful to them and to God that the opportunity to serve wasn't closed on him forever. The church responds to this renewed hopefulness, and the pastor starts feeling less alone. Together they start sensing a renewed passion to express Christ's love to people who aren't in their church. Soon, some fresh faces start arriving again.

Bitterness and anger don't disappear overnight, and some people still leave the church with the same old excuses, but it no longer carries the personal sting of failure like it used to. Since guilt has been removed as his primary motivation for ministry, he starts taking occasional weekends off with the family. The church does fine when he's gone, and instead of feeling threatened by that, he's relieved. Mending fences with his wife isn't easy, but with help, prayer and hard work that starts getting better too.

After a few years into this new phase of life, he starts realizing something he hasn't felt for a while. He's actually happy! He feels content with who he is and what he's been called to do in the body of Christ. He's discovered who he *is* called to be by abandoning what he *isn't* called to be.

The joy is greater and the burden is lighter.

Stage 7 – Fulfillment & Effectiveness

He feels reborn. His first love is restored.

He'll never be that idealistic young pastor again, but he is finally living up to his true, deeper ideals. The work of the ministry becomes less stressful, more joyful and more fulfilling. As a result, he's more effective at what he does. He's even become willing to try doing ministry in fresh, innovative ways. Not to keep up with trends, but because real ministry just requires that kind of original thinking sometimes.

He no longer desires the things he used to think he could never do without. Bigger crowds, the praise of his peers and a reputation for being a trend-setter are no longer on his radar. Instead, he finds new depths in God's Word and new joys in friendships (*actual friendships!*) within the church. He gets to know his unchurched neighbors, not out of some sense of duty, but from a sincere desire to connect with them and love them.

Soon, people in the church and others that he never thought would have an interest in spiritual things, start being drawn to him. More one-on-one and face-to-face than in organized groups. There's just something about him that people feel like they can learn from.

People use words like *genuine* and *approachable* when they refer to him. He spends more time in conversations over coffee, and less time in ministerial conferences and seminars.

Then one day a young, wide-eyed couple walks into his church. They have become engaged while attending a local seminary and they feel a call to enter pastoral ministry when they graduate. They want to learn and to help, and have heard this might be a great place to add some hands-on practical experience to their academic training, and explore new ideas in an accepting environment. The pastor smiles and invites the couple into his office. As they sit on his couch, they have a look of anticipation and excitement in their eyes. As he finds a seat facing them, the older pastor breathes in deeply.

What is that? Ah yes.

That new car smell.

Chapter 13

What Do Small Church Pastors Want and Need?

The undeclared Small Church / Big Church turf war has gone on long enough. The casualties are everywhere. It's time for a truce.

We're not enemies. We're not even supposed to be competitors. So we need to stop acting like we are.

If you're a big church pastor, you need to know that Small Church pastors need your help. But we're not charity cases. You need our help too.

More than anything else, Small Church pastors would like to hear and see more evidence of what we know is in the hearts of our peers in ministry. That we matter to God. To our communities. To the church as a whole. To our denominations. And to the kingdom of God.

Here are three simple ways you can let us know we're working together on this.

#1. An Honest Assessment of the Task

I've noticed two opposite but equally problematic tendencies from some megachurch pastors and church growth teachers in the way they explain how to build a big church, and how they built theirs.

I'll call the first one, the "I have no idea how it happened" approach, while the other is the "here's exactly how to do it" approach. What both tendencies have in common is that they make church growth seem easier than it is.

The "I have no idea how it happened" approach involves the tendency to underplay the amount of hard work and unique skills it takes to build a big church. Rob Bell did this, unintentionally I believe, in *Velvet Elvis*. As he tells it, they started the church thinking, "if thirteen people joined up with us, and that was all it ever was, that would be okay." And I have no doubt he meant that. Then the first Sunday came and ... over 1,000 people showed up! Within a month or two it grew to over 2,000 and within six months it was over 4,000.

Four thousand new church-attenders in six months is awesome, amazing, almost unprecedented growth. But every pastor who reads Bell's story knows that such explosive growth didn't come so easily – or surprisingly. Something was left out of the story.

For instance, when 1,000 people showed up on the first Sunday, there's no mention of having to turn anyone away from the building. If you were anticipating thirteen people, why would you rent a facility that accommodates over 1,000? Somebody was expecting something. And they were prepared for it. I'm glad they were.

Megachurch pastors, I know you're trying to be humble, but it doesn't help the struggling Small Church pastor when we read or hear accounts that your church grew mega-big overnight simply because, "all we cared about was trying to teach and live the way of Jesus". That's what *we're* doing too! But it's not making our churches any bigger. So you must be doing something in addition to that.

Be transparent with us. Tell us about your hard work, your unique gift-blend, the 300 tithers who came with you from your mothering church, the ministry team member who had strengths where you were weak, the pre-built audience from your days in a local rock band, etc.

The combination of skills, gifts, circumstances, wisdom, work, anointing, calling and God's timing that are required to grow a church to large or mega size is simply staggering. And that is at least one reason why there are so few large churches and so many small ones.

The second megachurch pastor teaching method is the "here's exactly how to do it" approach. Instead of underplaying the required gift mix, this method overplays the likelihood that anyone can grow a big church if we just follow a particular set of guidelines.

So we read the books and go to the seminars, then head back home excited about the expected church growth that's now going to happen for us, only to find ourselves more discouraged than ever when the "inevitable" doesn't happen. Then we wonder – if this technique worked for the pastor who taught it and for all those other pastors who came on stage with their church growth testimonies, *what's wrong with me?*

The answer? Probably nothing is wrong with you.

My dad pastored for 45 years, mostly in mid- to large-sized churches. His response to the dilemma of the what-worked-for-you-isn't-working-for-me syndrome is, "God doesn't sell franchises". In other words, church isn't like McDonald's. You can't take the same systems from one place and plug-and-play them in another place.

God has this annoying tendency to do things his way, not ours. While the principles of his way never change, the methods and results are always different in every place and for every church and pastor.

There is no one-size-fits-all solution for growing churches.

When megachurch pastors and church growth teachers imply that building a big church is either so simple that anyone can do it or that it's so mysterious they don't know why it happened for them, it leaves the rest of us in the dark.

The bottom line is this – building a megachurch is very hard work, on the level of assembling a Super Bowl-winning NFL team or building a Fortune 500 company. The gift-mix required to do it is extremely rare. All the books and seminars in the world won't change what a person's gifts are. No amount of prayer, passion, planning or great Bible teaching will turn a church that's supposed to be a Small Church into a megachurch. Or a Small Church pastor into a megachurch pioneer.

Megachurch pastors, it's not less-than-humble to tell us how you did it. When you tell us your story, please tell us how your church growth really happened, including the non-repeatable hand-of-God moments. If you know how certain things came to be, tell us. If other things were a complete out-of-the-blue shock, let us know that too. At least then, when we see the uniqueness of each situation we can start admitting that megachurch growth isn't meant for every church.

Megachurch mega-growth has always been for a very small percentage of churches and pastors. Can we all just admit that and be OK with it?

#2. Acknowledge Our Struggles

While no two churches are alike, including no two Small Churches, there are some struggles that most Small Churches share, and I seldom hear them addressed. Here are just two of them:

Under-representation
Small Church pastors tend to struggle alone. Many of us can't

afford to go to conferences to learn new ideas and meet with fellow pastors for moral support. Many denominations offer some assistance to the Small Church pastors who need these conferences, but some offer none at all. So the conferences become over-represented by larger churches and under-represented by smaller ones.

This was one of the premises of another Malcolm Gladwell book, *Outliers.* In it, he notes a well-documented Canadian study that shows kids born in January tend to make better grades and score more goals in sports than those born later in the year. The reason, he deduces, is that grade-school kids who were born just after the cut-off date for the school year (January) are always a year older than the kids who were born just before it (December), thus having a full year of mental and physical advantages.

The January kids aren't naturally brighter and more physically capable than kids born in November and December. They're just a year older. In elementary school, one year is a lot.

The school system doesn't see that, so the January kids get labeled as gifted, while the December kids are called slow. Once established, those categories are hard to break out of. The gifted kids get enrolled in advanced classes, increasing the pace of their education and making the gap between them and the December kids bigger.

The physically larger January kids are recruited by better PeeWee teams, then better High Schools and colleges. That's why, as shown in Gladwell's book, professional sports leagues – and hockey leagues in particular – have an inordinately high percentage of athletes that were born in the first three months of the year and a much lower percentage of December birthdays.

Interestingly, Gladwell calls this phenomenon *The Matthew Effect,* from Jesus' words in Matthew 25:29, "For everyone who has will be given more, and he will have an abundance. Whoever does not have, even what he has will be taken from him."

The Matthew Effect may be happening in the church. Once your church has been labeled small in a church culture that sees being small as a problem, it's hard to break free from it. That's why the longer a church stays small, the more likely it is to remain small. Pastoral seminars, by their very nature, appeal to pastors of larger churches because they can afford the enrollment fees and they don't have to take time off from a secular job to be there. The Small Church pastor suffers under *The Matthew Effect.* If he finds himself a year behind, especially early on, that's where he's likely to stay.

For the bi-vocational pastor it's even harder. They're seldom able go to conferences, shoot a round of golf or even grab a cup of coffee with a fellow pastor. They spend their weeks working at UPS, their weekends at church. Even if someone were to subsidize their entire conference fee, they can't afford several days off from their paying job plus the cost of gas, food and lodging. The conference will burn up their vacation days, shortening the time they can spend with the family again this year.

The Need for Rest
When I was burned out and needed a break I was blessed to have a church that was loving enough and stable enough to let me walk away for forty days to get some much-needed rest and recovery.

Whenever I've told other pastors that I just walked away from the church for forty days, I typically hear one of two reactions, both fear-based.

Reaction #1: "I could never do that! The church would fall apart if I was gone for forty days!"

Reaction #2: "I could never do that! What if they found out they can run the church without me?"

Forty days. Are most churches really just forty days away from either falling apart or replacing their pastor?

Then I go to pastoral seminars and I hear how important it is to take time away from the church for several weeks every year, and several months of sabbatical at least every five years or so. I agree, especially after my experiences with burnout, that those break times are essential for effectiveness and longevity in ministry.

There are megachurch pastors who have taught that a part of the reason for their success in ministry is that they take forty days or so annually to get spiritually refreshed, re-cast vision and/or write sermons for the coming year. They recommend that others do the same.

I recommend it too. But forty days off for rest or sermon prep is a laughable pipe-dream for most pastors. When many of them read or hear such advice, their reaction is often to feel even more disenchantment, resentment and feelings of disconnection from their fellow pastors.

I'm not saying any of this to complain, and if it sounds petty I apologize. I'm letting these issues be known here because I've never heard them stated anywhere outside the occasional private conversation when Small Church pastors get together.

We whisper them to each other.

It's time to state them out loud.

We can't fix what we won't admit.

#3. Recognize Our Unique Needs and Contributions

Just as every church growth story is unique, so is every Small Church story. But, while each church has distinctive elements, we can also learn common principles. That's why we read books and go to seminars.

Take a look at who's speaking at the church leadership seminars. Seriously, right now, go to the internet and look up almost any pastoral ministry conference or seminar. When they list the bio of the pastor who's speaking, the first line is almost always about the size of their church, and usually how quickly it got to that size. If the speaker isn't a megachurch pastor or evangelist, it'll be someone who's done research or written about megachurches. It's about time somebody told the people who put these conferences on, that putting such stats front-and-center can discourage as many Small Church pastors as they encourage.

Can anyone remember the last time the pastor of a Small Church was asked to teach at one of these seminars on the principles unique to leading a Small Church? Or was invited to sit on a panel with pastors of various church sizes to talk about how we can work together?

Big church pastors are the ones teaching the seminars and writing the books. Certainly some of the principles of pastoring a Small Church overlap with pastoring a big one, and yes, we need to know how to grow from one stage of numerical growth to another. But most megachurch principles are exclusive to megachurches and will never apply in my church. And it's not always easy to figure out which is which.

As a Small Church pastor, I need another Small Church pastor to teach me most of the principles that can help me do my job better.

Megachurch pastors aren't teaching me how to pastor a church, they're teaching me how to pastor a megachurch. That's understandable, because that's what they know. But they need to realize that when they talk megachurch they're speaking the language of a very small segment of the audience. Someone needs to do the hard work of sniffing out some good, local Small Church pastors and have at least one of them, or a panel of them, make presentations or be a part of the discussions at pastoral leadership seminars.

I don't expect Small Church pastors to be the lead speakers at these conferences. If I'm going to pony up a $200 fee to attend, it's because I saw Craig Groeschel's face on the flyer, not pastor Karl Unknown from First Small Church of Nowhereville. As we've already talked about, most Small Church pastors can't afford to go to the seminars anyway. But we need to start paying more attention to these issues than we have been. Any revitalization of the body of Christ will require everyone to be involved with each body part contributing to the whole.

These attitude shifts won't take place overnight, but I'd like to offer one idea for a spark that could start something very special.

Chapter 14
Just One City

Imagine a city of one million people.

The churches in it might break down in size like this:

- 4 megachurches averaging ...... 5,000, ... for a total of 20,000
- 15 big churches 1,000 15,000
- 40 mid-size churches 500 20,000
- 100 semi-small churches 250 25,000
- 500 Small Churches 100 50,000
- 500 house churches ....15................. 7,500
- For a total church attendance of 137,500

Which church size is the *most* essential to this city?

The *least* essential?

It should be obvious by now that we need all of them.

We need everyone operating in the best possible way in a cooperative spirit of mutual aid and appreciation. Anything less than that will never help the church break out of its static place as a mostly forgotten subsection of overall city life, cut off from any sense of connection to the needs and psyche of the city, not to mention from each other.

Divide and conquer. It's a primary battle strategy. There may be no more effective strategy being used today against the church. The tragedy is that the wounds are entirely self-inflicted.

I don't expect the principles you've just read about to be heralded in cities around the world in some kind of global renaissance. But here's a thought.

What if just one city decided to give it a shot?

It doesn't have to be a city of a million. That's just a nice, round number to work with. It could be a suburb, an agricultural community or a huge metropolis. But what do you think God might do through a city whose pastors and churches decided they were finally going to set aside their territorialism, their petty jealousies and their denominational prejudices?

What If

What if, instead of despising our differences or ignoring them, we started celebrating them? And started utilizing the benefits of them?

What if Small Church pastors started naming the grasshopper myth for the lie that it is and started accepting the truth – that their church *at its current size* is exactly where God wants it to be. Some of them will stay that size, some will grow, but...

What if they took the Apostle Paul's encouragement to heart, and could truly say, "I have learned the secret of being content in any and every situation..." Wouldn't such "godliness with contentment" result in "great gain" for the kingdom of God?

What if all the pastors in this city decided to stop crowing about how big they are or whining about how small they are, and decided they would find and do God's will for their specific size, in their city, borough, neighborhood, block or apartment complex?

What if megachurches held free seminars with speakers specifically targeted at helping small and mid-size churches get the tools they need?

What if Small Churches kept a list of the help groups offered at nearby big- to megachurches for recovery, counseling, mid-week Bible Study, etc. so that the people who attend their churches for weekend worship, but need ministry during the week that their Small Church isn't equipped to provide, can go to one of these other churches for help, guilt-free?

What if big churches realized they have things to learn and blessings to receive from Small Churches too? Re-gaining intimacy and letting go of some institutionalization might be a place to start.

What if pastors in churches of all sizes felt released to receive personal benefit from the ministries of other local churches when they needed spiritual sustenance themselves?

What if big churches were open to help Small Church pastors when they were ill, burnt out or simply needed a vacation, by doing things like offering to send one of their teaching pastors to speak on a weekend service, free of charge, with a promise not to proselytize?

What if this kind of practical, hands-on, church-to-church loving of one another as Christ loved us started being noticed by a city that's running short on real, loving relationships? Wouldn't that be a better way for them to know we are Christ's followers than a city-wide billboard campaign?

What if there was **Just One City** in the world that gave this a shot?

I know this is idealistic, naïve, pie-in-the-sky thinking.

But what if it *isn't*?

What if we at least *tried* this?

What if it started with *your* city?

What if it started with *you*?

Wouldn't God be pleased with those efforts?

And if he was pleased...

What if it *worked*?

Those churches could change that city.

And that city would change the world.

Chapter 15

Becoming an Ex-Grasshopper

Now what?

I hope you've been inspired and challenged by God to take a fresh look at your church and your ministry.

But how exactly do we implement these principles and move from Grasshopper to Ex-Grasshopper?

After all, I've thrown a lot at you. Thirty-plus years of failures and successes, learning and growing, challenging presumptions and pointing to new possibilities. And I still have a whole lifetime of learning ahead of me.

Wouldn't it be nice if we could take all of that and turn it into doable steps? Not a roadmap for the rest of life, of course, but how about a starting point or two?

That's what God did for the Hebrews. After their involuntary forty year Grasshopperectomy they were finally ready to take the land, so God gave them a first step. Literally. Take a walk around Jericho today, he told them. Then do it again the next day. And the next.

I'd like to offer four starter steps that helped me. You'll recognize the essence of each of them from the previous pages.

They aren't necessarily in the best order for you. They aren't even in the order I did them. Step four came first for me. But they are in a logical, if not chronological order. You'll probably end up working on more than one at a time, so I suggest starting with the one that seems easiest.

I've tried to make these as doable as possible by gathering as many helpful tools as I can on my blog at NewSmallChurch.com, all in one place, free of charge. If you go there, you'll find some practical help, encouragement, feedback and community.

If you're ready to move from Grasshopper to Ex-Grasshopper, the good news is there's no need to go charging alone through the gates. At least not yet. Maybe never.

For now, let's take a look at some important first steps around the walls of Jericho.

Step #1: Get Brutally Honest

There is no strategy to freedom. No program. No shortcuts.

Just the truth.

It's the only way to break free from The Grasshopper Myth. And, as always, Jesus said it best.

> *"If you hold to my teaching, you are really my disciples. Then you will know the truth, and the truth will set you free." – John 8:31-32*

Hold to Jesus' teaching. Believe what he says about you, your ministry, your past and your future.

Know the truth.

Freedom starts here.

Be Honest with God

Sometimes I wonder if we've learned anything since Adam and Eve sewed fig leaves together and hid among the trees. We still spend too much of our lives putting on our Sunday Best for God, only to run and hide when he shows up because we know the leaves don't cover anything that matters.

We need to stand fig-leaf-free before a holy God. Get used to investing time with him again. Re-activate that long-dormant prayer life. Re-ignite a thirst for God's Word rather than just going to it for sermon material.

It's time to fall in love with Jesus again.

Ironically, when we hide from God we're hiding from the only one who knows more about us than we know about ourselves. From the one who loves us anyway. If honesty doesn't start here, it can't happen anywhere.

Be Honest with Yourself

Self-deceit is the core of The Grasshopper Myth. If you still feel like a grasshopper, admit it to God and yourself. It's not a lack of faith to confess the truth.

Then look at the bigger truth. What is truer – that you feel like a grasshopper, or that God says you're not one?

Be Honest with Your "Family"

I put "family" in quotes here, because this could be your biological family or your emotional and spiritual family – or a combination of both. For some of us, they don't overlap.

The people who are closest to you probably already know most of the truths you've tried to hide. They may have been trying to tell you for years. The secrets you think will shock them may be met with nods of relief to see that you're finally owning up to it.

Be Honest with Your Ministry Team

I don't know your ministry team. They may not be safe people for you. Many of you can't expose yourself to your church leadership like I described in Chapter 2. Not yet, at least. They may not be ready to handle certain truths. And you may not be in a good place to tell them.

Remember Chapter Two where I told you how excited I used to get after reading ministry books? Please don't do that with this book. Don't go storming in to tell your board and/or staff that a book called The Grasshopper Myth is the answer for your church. They may think you've joined a cult. Plus, it's not the answer. Only Jesus is.

Don't... (I can't believe I'm writing this...) Please *don't* go online and buy ten copies for your leadership team to read until you are absolutely sure they're prepared to hear what it says.

Let it simmer in your spirit for a while. Maybe re-read it. Slowly and prayerfully this time.

If your ministry team isn't prepared to discuss this yet, that's OK. You weren't ready for a long time either. For now, jump down a few paragraphs and find out what it means to share what's brewing in your spirit with some safe people. People who "get it".

After it simmers for a while and starts bubbling up organically in your life (*now* I can say it...) *then* go online and buy copies for your leaders. Schedule a Saturday to talk about it after they've read it. Or take a couple months to go through it chapter-by-chapter one night a week. That's what the Discussion Guide is for.

In the meantime, like I said, I don't know your leadership team, so I can't tell you what's safe to share with them.

But I do know this. Stop lying to them. Now.

Stop pretending you have the answers when you don't. Stop burning so much energy putting on a false front. Quit saying, "God told me" when he didn't. They're all just fig leaves.

It may take a while to get to the *whole* truth, but you'll never get there if you don't start with *the truth and nothing but the truth*. So help you God.

Be Honest with Someone Who Can Help You
I told you about my visits to a counselor in Chapter Two. If your grasshopper hasn't dug in as deeply as mine, you may not need professional help. If it's dug in deeper, you may need more. A lot more.

If you need help, get it. There may be some good local counselors who provide help for free or at a reduced rate. If not, there may be funding for counseling through your denomination. If you have to pay for it out of your own pocket, *pay for it!* The cost of not getting the help you need is far greater than any money you will spend.

This next point should be obvious, but I'll say it anyway.

Make sure, make absolutely certain, that the therapist or counselor is a Bible-believing Christian who uses scriptural truths as the unshakable foundation of their practice. Don't just ask about their church attendance or look for a seminary degree on the wall. This is your mind, your spirit, your ministry and your life. Don't entrust them to anyone who isn't entrusting their mind, spirit, ministry and life to Jesus too.

Be Honest with People Who "Get It"
We all know what "it" is, right? No, I can't describe "it" any better than you can. We just know when it's there and we sense when it's missing.

It's about connection, empathy, common goals and visions. About people who say what we've always felt, even before we knew we felt them. It's being able to finish each other's sentences while spurring each other to better things.

Finding others that "get it" doesn't necessarily mean they get *you*. After all, you may not have gotten yourself for a long time now.

Start by seeking out pastors in your town or denomination who've had helpful ministry experiences. Not the ones with all the successes and all the answers. You've tried that already. Instead, find people who've shared common struggles. Find a Stage Seven pastor (from Chapter 12, *The Emotional Life of the Small Church Pastor*) and pour out your heart.

Or find people who've read this book. At least you'll have that in common. Chat about what you liked and hated about it and what each of you plans to do next.

If there's no one nearby you can do that with, or if you're just not ready for something that intimate yet, that's one reason I set up NewSmallChurch.com.

Step #2: Determine Who You're NOT

Kill the grasshopper.

Bury its dead, rotting carcass deep in an unmarked desert grave on the far side of the Jordan.

But know this. It's a stubborn little beast. It won't die easily. It can't be wished away or even prayed away. Although prayer is an essential part of this.

Life doesn't go where you *want* it to go – it goes where you *tell* it to go. And you tell it where to go with every decision you make – large and small.

Stop making grasshopper choices. Stop living on defense. Say "no" to saying "no".

Your biggest problem in ministry and in life isn't that you'll make a mistake, but that you'll be consumed by the *fear* of making a mistake. That's what happened to the ten faithless Hebrew spies. The giants and walls they saw weren't bigger than the ones Joshua and Caleb saw. Their biggest challenges weren't external, they were internal. They couldn't see they weren't slaves any more.

It's one of the oldest sayings in history. It's easier to take the people out of Egypt than it is to take Egypt out of the people. That's where The Grasshopper Myth started.

I began discovering who I'm not on the day I told my staff, "We need to stop thinking like a big church." I didn't know who I *was* yet. But removing the burden of who I was *not* was one of the most liberating experiences of my life.

If you're not sure who you *are* yet, that's OK. Start by declaring who you're *not*.

Step #3: Discover Who You ARE

It's time to redefine success. To be OK with who you are and where you are.

Are you a Small Church Pastor? Say it.

Seriously. Right now. Get past the awkward feelings and *say* it.

"I'm _____ and I'm a Small Church pastor."

If you've looked at the back cover of this book, or if you've been to NewSmallChurch.com, you've seen a picture of me holding a nametag towards the camera. The statement, "Hi, I'm Karl and I'm a

Small Church Pastor," is on the nametag. Not coincidentally, it's also the title of the first chapter.

That photo is not about me. It's about all of us. It's a declaration that you and I are not grasshoppers.

We are Small Church pastors, not because we failed at being big church pastors, but because this is what God called us to do and who he gifted us to be.

I'd like you to join me in that declaration.

Sometimes we *discover* who we are, only after *declaring* who we are.

Yes, I'm going to ask you to go to NewSmallChurch.com again. This time, look for the Nametag Wall. When you do, you'll find a photo gallery of people, just like you and me, who downloaded a nametag, wrote their name on it in big, bold letters, took a picture of themselves holding it, then sent the photo to us.

I'd love to add your photo to this growing community of self-identified Small Church pastors and friends.

No, a photo and a nametag won't change your life or your ministry. But the declaration behind it might be a first step.

Which leads us to...

Step #4: Start DOING It – Whatever It Is

It's much easier to educate a doer than it is to activate a thinker.
– Andy Stanley

Doing something right is more important than doing nothing wrong.
– Erwin MacManus

Sometimes the secret to getting things done is just to do them.
– Oliver Burkeman

Do or do not. There is no try. – Yoda

You're a thinker and a reader. Me too.

That's good. Things that don't start with thinking and reading usually don't start well. I've also discovered that anything that ends with thinking and reading – ends before it begins.

There comes a time when you have to lay the book down, stop thinking, talking and planning, and start doing. You'll never have all the steps planned out in advance. Sometimes you won't have the first step planned out. Step out anyway.

The water of the Jordan didn't roll back until the priests got their feet wet. Sometimes you have to drown your grasshopper.

Doing something is scary. It puts us out there. It requires faith – actual, practical, risky faith.

You know those moments when you're feeling especially brave and smart? The next time you feel that way, even a little bit, start writing. Write down your dreams, goals, ideas, action steps, everything. Just pour your heart onto a blank page.

Then, the next time you're not feeling brave and smart, don't let it paralyze you. Work the list.

As an example, the title of this book was a big risk for me. I ran through dozens of titles before landing on this one. All the others were safer and made more sense. At some point almost every chapter title was a possible book title, then it was The New Small Church, then Discovering The New Small Church... You get the idea.

One day I was feeling especially brave and smart, so I started writing new ideas down. I asked myself, not what would be a correct title, but what would be the title of a ministry book I'd want to read?

For reasons I don't even remember anymore, the grasshopper story from the book of Numbers kept coming up. I downloaded an image of a grasshopper to my laptop and played with how it might look on a book cover. I experimented with grasshopper titles. When I put The Grasshopper Myth on the cover, I liked it.

Then it started scaring me. Brave and smart were suddenly nowhere to be found.

I sat on that title for a while before mentioning it to anyone. I wanted to run back to previous titles – safer ones.

Then I did something essential. I borrowed some courage. I talked to some brave friends. It turned out they loved it, grasshopper and all.

We all know who our brave friends are and who our safe friends are. We need both in our lives. There are times we need to talk to our safe friends – when we're considering getting married after three dates, for instance. Then there are times when we need to talk to our brave friends. Not the stupid ones – not the one who push us into things.

Never listen to the pushers.

Listen to the pullers.

Listen to the ones who know and love us – who see the best, bravest parts of us. The ones who get out there in admirable ways. The ones who aren't afraid to fail. The ones who pull us to come with them.

The pushers force us to go against our will to places they'd never go, then they leave us standing alone, exposed and naked.

The pullers draw us to where they're going. They tap into our God-given desire for adventure and joy. Then they walk through it with us.

If you don't have any pullers in your life, I encourage you to find some. Start with other Ex-Grasshoppers. Meet us online if you don't know where else to start. Start by peeking in on the conversation. Then join in when you're ready.

The End of the Myth

A book and a website can't get you to where you need to go. No matter how many times you read, re-read, study, discuss or even teach others the principles you've learned, they won't change your life or ministry one little bit. You have to actually do the stuff.

You have to start.

Somewhere, at some time, you have to take that first step.

Your somewhere is here.

Your sometime is now.

You're not a grasshopper.

And that's no myth.

Discussion Guide

The Grasshopper Myth is meant to stir us to action. Sometimes the starting point for that action is meaningful discussion. Online, at ministerial meetings and in our churches.

This chapter-by-chapter guide is included to help jump-start those discussions. The questions in this guide may also help some readers review and assess their personal responses to the issues raised. Some may want to use it to initiate personal reflection and renewal in prayer.

Use it in whatever way works for you.

Introductory Pages

Have you ever felt the symptoms of The Grasshopper Myth in your own ministry? Do you feel it now? How does it feel to have it diagnosed?

What situations have you allowed to enter your life that have made you feel like a grasshopper in ministry? What will you do to stop believing the lie?

1. Hi, I'm Karl and I'm a Small Church Pastor

Have you ever felt like a failure in ministry? If so, where did the Grasshopper Myth begin for you? What did that sense of failure cause you to do, or not do?

What does the Eleanor Roosevelt quote, "No one can make you feel inferior without your consent" mean to you? Have you ever given that consent to anyone?

Has the drive for "butts in the seats and bucks in the offering" ever been a temptation for you?

Do you agree or disagree with the statement, "This drive for greater numbers and larger churches has probably resulted in more pastoral burnout than healthy, growing churches?" Why?

Do you believe there is an optimal size for every church at which they are likely to stop growing numerically and need to find other ways to grow? If so, what might that look like for your church?

What do you think about the difference between a healthy church and a healthful one?

Why do so many people choose to attend Small Churches, even when there are big ones available?

The author says he wants to get a conversation started. Is this a conversation you'd like to be in on? (If you'd like to get in on such a conversation, go to NewSmallChurch.com and look around).

2. How Trying to Build a Big Church Nearly Killed Me – and My Church

What did your spiritual journey toward Christ look like? How does it influence the way you minister today?

Have you had any experiences with the teachings of the church growth movement? What were they like?

What have you had to unlearn about how to do ministry? What do you need to unlearn still?

What was your biggest strategic mistake in ministry?

Have you ever been through emotional or spiritual valleys in ministry? What caused them and how did you get through them?

Have you ever felt like God let you down? How did you deal with it?

The author received great grace from his church leadership team when he admitted his failings. Has this been your experience? If so, what did it mean to you? If not, what effect did it have on you?

Have you ever hurt someone in ministry? Have you sought forgiveness and reconciliation? If so, how did it go? If not, what's holding you back?

Have you ever had to "redefine success"? If so, how did that work? Do you have to do that in your ministry now? If so, what steps will you take to get there?

Have you ever experienced the overwhelming joy of grace from another person? What was the experience like for you?

Have you ever had bad emotional or spiritual habits that have tried to come back after they were gone? How did you deal with that?

3. Stop Thinking Like a Big Church

Can you relate to the statement, "I wasn't called to manage systems. I was called to pastor people"? Do your ministry style and your gifts lean more towards being a rancher or a shepherd? Which one does your church most need you to be right now?

Do you agree with the author that many of the methods we've used in the church in the last half-century may have come from military and industrial principles more than from scripture?

If you're a pastor, have you ever felt like you had to justify your choices to be a caregiving shepherd rather than an administrative rancher? Or vise versa?

Do you believe megachurch pastors have a unique burden to bear?

Have you ever considered the different styles and methods of ministry that are needed for churches of different sizes? What type of church are you ministering in, and what adaptations to your ministry style might you need to make?

Why do you think there has been so much written about house churches and megachurches, but so little about the vast majority of churches that land somewhere in between? Have you read other helpful books on Small Churches? (If you have read helpful books or know of other good sources on this subject, please go to NewSmallChurch.com and tell us about it).

4. Don't Despise the Size

Have you ever felt like others look down on you or your church because it's small? How much responsibility do you take for allowing yourself to feed those feelings?

Have you ever had unbiblical attitudes towards big churches and/or their pastors? Is this something you need to correct? If so, how?

Can a small church be a great church? Have you ever considered that possibility before? If not, why not?

Is being OK with a church's small size just an excuse for settling for mediocrity? If so, why? If not, why not?

What do you think about the idea that Small Churches perform some of the functions in the body of Christ that small groups fulfill in big churches?

The author states, "A lot of Small Churches are not very good, and that's why they're small." Do you agree or disagree? Will you accept the author's challenge to discover and fix ways that your church may not be doing all that it can do?

5. Why We Need Churches of All Sizes

What do you think about the parable comparing the styles of IKEA and Starbucks? Do you think church leaders have made that mistake in their perception of Small Churches?

As a church leader, have you ever been guilty of telling people how important their gifts are, while devaluing your own gifts, or those of your church?

How much of the value of being in a Small Church comes from being "a participant in the process, not a customer"?

"One of the reasons people go to Small Churches is that its smaller size allows them to have a more personal stake in what happens. They know they matter." Do you agree? If so, what can your church do to help people know they matter even more?

6. So What's Wrong with Church Growth?

Do you agree with the author's claim that too many churches are "growth-oriented, not health-oriented"? What about your church?

Have you ever been guilty of the presumption that it is a problem for a church to be small? Where do you think that presumption comes from?

What would change about your church and your ministry if you took the advice from *Soar With Your Strengths* and started concentrating on doing what you're good at instead of focusing on fixing what you're not good at?

How long has it been since you thought about where your church fits within the larger body of Christ? What would it mean to rediscover that place again?

"Let's stop arguing about which size is best, and start seeing what's best about each size." What would that mean for you and your church?

7. Only In a Small Church

How important is it to the people in your church to have access to the pastor? If you're a pastor, is that something you enjoy or do you find it a challenge? Maybe a little of both?

If you're a pastor, do you relate to the author's desire to be a member of your church, not just its leader? Are you able to do that now? If not, what are some steps you can take to move towards that?

Do you think people are craving for more intimacy in their worship experience, or less? What can your Small Church do to create an environment that is both intimate and accountable, while also being emotionally and spiritually safe?

"I want to be a part of a worship experience that requires my participation rather than encouraging passivity." Do you agree or disagree with that? How well is your church doing that? Are there ways the team can work together to improve that?

"Availability needs a training ground if it is going to become ability."
Has your church created an environment where people can learn,
make mistakes and grow? If not, why not? What needs to be done
to change that?

Were you aware that so many historical revolutions were sparked in
Small Churches? Does that help change your perspective about what
kind of impact a Small Church can have?

8. Small Church, Big Vision

"The New Small Church is not about timid little churches." Do you
think Small Churches have been stereotyped in that way? Has your
church? What would it mean for your church to break out of that?

"Thinking small is not the same as *small thinking*. And it's definitely
not an excuse for having a small vision." What's the difference
between *thinking small* and *small thinking*? Is this a distinction that
can help you and your church develop a big vision?

What does it mean for you to have "godliness with contentment" in
ministry?

"God didn't call me to pastor *that* church, he called me to pastor *this*
one." Is that true for you? If so, what implications does that have for
your future ministry?

What can your church bring to your community that no one else
can? If you know what that is, are you doing it? If not, what can you
do to discover it?

"Fear keeps more churches on the defense than anything else." Do
you agree? What can you do to overcome that fear?

"Churches on defense put up signs. Churches on offense put up
ramps." What "signs" does your church put up, maybe without
realizing it? What "ramps" could you replace them with?

"Many Small Churches have given up innovation for survival – offense for defense." What does that mean for you and your church?

"Our budget dictates our theology." "Our marketing choices dictate our theology." "Our janitorial schedule dictates our theology." Do you agree or disagree that those things happen? What are the implications of it for your ministry?

Do you agree that the structures of the church that were meant to enhance ministry, sometimes hinder it? Does that issue need to be addressed in your ministry?

Do you relate to "Our church building may be small, but our vision, our ministry and our reputation doesn't have to be"? Are there innovative ways to use your church facility, or to do ministry outside the building that you can explore?

Do you agree that "worshipping only with people who look like us is not healthy or biblical"?

Has your church relied more on "Go into…" strategies or "Come and see"? Does there need to be some adjustment to that balance?

9. An Open Letter – To My Fellow Small Church Pastors

Have you ever considered how many people around the world attend a Small Church every week? What does that say to you about the value of Small Church ministry?

What benefits have you and your church received from the ministries of megachurch pastors?

Would you like to give and receive support from other Small Church ministries? Have you reached out to any ministries to build or strengthen those ties?

10. God Doesn't Take Attendance

What are some things pastors and church leaders can do to re-emphasize the message that church attendance is a means to an end, not the end-game for Christians?

"Some pastors count people because some pastors count everything! That's who they are. They're numbers-oriented. That's how God made them..." Are you primarily numbers-oriented or people oriented? What are you doing to capitalize on those traits?

Jesus told us to "Love God. Love others. That's all." If we stopped to remember that more often, how would it change the way we minister?

How important is it to recognize that Jesus builds his church, not us? How encouraging is it to realize that the local church is a vital part of an amazing work that Jesus has done, is doing and will continue to do until he comes?

Is it possible that your church is at its optimal size right now? If not, what size would be optimal? Why?

What do you think of the statement, "it's not healthy, godly or helpful to push a church to places God isn't asking it to go in order to meet some artificial numerical standard or stroke the pastor's ego. Even if we call it faith."

11. A New Way to Define Success

"I think we should measure success the way Jesus did... One person at a time. Are individual people growing? Is the community being impacted? That's what matters." Do you agree or disagree? Do you have any concerns about doing ministry that way?

How important is it for church leaders to rely on what Helmut Thielicke called, "the spiritual instinct of the children of God"?

Do you believe you can have true success in ministry without numbers to back it up? If so, are there ways to keep track of non-numerical success?

"If Jesus is doing the building and getting the credit, I should be just as thrilled when my efforts put someone into a healthy church down the street or around the world as I am when they come to the church I'm pastoring." How true is that for you and your church?

What are your thoughts about the author's premise that, instead of always trying to attract large crowds, Jesus often tried to avoid them? Why do you think Jesus did that?

In what ways does the current size of your congregation make it well-suited to minister to the community you're in?

Do you agree or disagree that "there is value in failure"? If so, what might some of that value be?

Why do you think the Bible gives us so few clues about the structure of the local church?

Are there ways your church can take advantage of the new "flat world" to do ministry?

"Small Churches are seldom smooth, corporate, institutional or cool. That may be one of the coolest things about them." Can you relate to that?

12. Stages in the Emotional Life of the Small Church Pastor

If you're a Small Church pastor, which emotional stage do you think you might be in right now?

Are you aware of any warning signs that you may be flirting with the pitfalls described in Stages Three or Four? Are there steps you can take to minimize or avoid those dangers?

If you're in Stages Three, Four or Five is there someone you can trust, be honest with and get help from?

Have you ever considered the need to redefine success in your ministry? What might that look like for you?

If you're a Stage Seven pastor, what can you do to reach back to pastors in earlier stages?

13. What Do Small Church Pastors Want and Need?

Have you ever sensed an unspoken battle between mega and Small Churches, their ministries and pastors? Where do you think that comes from? Have you ever contributed to it?

Have you ever been frustrated by either the "I have no idea how it happened" approach or the "here's exactly how to do it" approach to church growth?

Have you ever wondered, *"what's wrong with me?"* when church ministry doesn't go as expected? How do you deal with those feelings?

What's your response to the author's father's statement, "God doesn't sell franchises"? What implications does that have for your church and ministry?

Is it possible that you or your church have become victims of *The Matthew Effect?* If so, what can you do about it?

Do you have any ideas that might answer the question the author raised about how to allow greater access to pastoral conferences for Small Church and bi-vocational pastors? (If you have any ideas, please go to NewSmallChurch.com and tell us about them).

When was the last time you took some significant time away from ministry to renew and recoup spiritually and emotionally? Are you willing to talk with your church leadership about the practical steps to help make that happen?

What kinds of help would you like to receive at pastoral seminars and conferences that would speak to your specific needs in a Small Church? (If you have any ideas, please go to NewSmallChurch.com and tell us about them).

14. Just One City

Is the breakdown of church size in your city or town similar to the one that opens this chapter? What does it say to you about the value of the Small Churches in your community?

Do you believe God wants the kind of cooperative spirit mentioned in this chapter to occur among the churches in your community? If so, what is stopping God's plan from happening? What role might the Holy Spirit be asking you to play in bringing it about?

What fig-leaves have you used to hide from God? What will you do to get rid of them?

What lies have you told yourself? Are you ready to believe what God says, rather than what you feel?

15. Becoming an Ex-Grasshopper

Do you have an emotional or spiritual "family" that you can be honest with? Write their names down. Which ones can you talk with right now?

How much of this can you share with your ministry team? If they're not a safe place right now, what steps can you take to get them ready to be a safe place? If not, do you need to think about assembling a different ministry team?

What lies have you told your ministry team that you need to stop telling?

Do you need to talk to a professional? If so, where can you go to start a list of possible counselors and where will you find the means to pay for it?

Do you know a Stage Seven pastor you can talk to?

How will you kill your grasshopper? What will be the biggest challenges in getting it to stay dead?

Has your life been controlled by your fear of making a mistake? What steps do you need to take to overcome that fear?

Are your ready to declare who you are? Can you redefine success without settling for less?

What's harder for you? Thinking and reading? Or doing? Do you need to work on a better balance between them?

Are you going to start a "brave and smart list"?

Do you have any "pullers" in your life? If not, what will you do to reach out to some?

What will be your first step towards becoming an ex-grasshopper?

Notes

Notes

Endnotes

1. Hi, I'm Karl and I'm a Small Church Pastor

Page 2: *"No one can make you feel inferior without your consent."* – Though universally attributed to Eleanor Roosevelt, there is no definitive proof she ever said it. The sentiment of the quote is true, either way.

Page 4: *"...and I seemed like a grasshopper in my own eyes"* is a reference to how the ten of the Hebrew spies felt after exploring the promised land in Numbers 13:32-33.

Page 6: *"one body with many parts"* – 1 Corinthians 12:20

Page 10: *"...that there should be no division in the body, but that its parts should have equal concern for each other."* – 1 Corinthians 12:25

2. How Trying to Build a Big Church Nearly Killed Me – and My Church

(no notes)

3. Stop Thinking Like a Big Church

Page 28: *He even opened the book by dedicating it to the hard-working Small Church bi-vocational pastors, whom he calls, "the true heroes of the faith."* – Rick Warren, The Purpose Driven Church, pg 7

Page 30: *…when Jesus commissioned Peter, he told him "feed my sheep."* – John 21:17

Page 30: *The ranching model tells us that our primary focus needs to move from "doing the caring" to "develop and manage a system of care."* – Carl F. George, How to Break Church Growth Barriers, pg 19

Page 30: *People want to be pastored, not spiritually managed.* – From a lecture by Rev. Bill Dogterom at Vanguard University, Costa Mesa, California

Page 30: Moses & Jethro story – Exodus 18

Page 30: *"to prepare God's people for works of service."* – Ephesians 4:11-12

Page 31: All three instances of Jesus telling Peter to *"feed my sheep"* are taken from John 21:15-17

Page 32: *I'm still looking for a pastoral ministry seminar … think long and hard before abandoning the shepherd model entirely.* – I'm sure someone has done this, but I'm unaware of it. If you have, or if you know of someone who has taught this in print or online, please let me know at NewSmallChurch.com

Page 33: *"Thousands of people …. These are some of the people I love more than anyone else on the earth."* – Francis Chan. First minute of Crazy Love DVD – part 4

Page 34: *"count the cost"* – Luke 12:18-20; 14:28-30

Page 34: *"Your pastor may be the loneliest guy in your church and*

unless you are him that probably doesn't make much sense at all." –
Mark Driscoll. May 21, 2012, www.Twitter.com/PastorMark

Page 34: *"Church incorporated"* – Rob Bell, Velvet Elvis, pg 104

Page 34: *...he wasn't prepared to handle it.* – Rob Bell, Velvet Elvis,
Movement Four, Tassels

Page 36: The categories of church personality shifts by size are the
result of consolidating ideas from various sources including Sizing
up the Congregation, by Arlin Routhauge; and The Small Church IS
Different!, By Lyle E. Schaller.

4. Don't Despise the Size

Page 39: *Size matters not. Look at me. Judge me by size, do you?* –
Yoda – Star Wars V: The Empire Strikes Back

Page 41: *"At the 100 mark ... 95 percent."* – Carl F. George, How to
Break Church Growth Barriers

Page 41: *...far more than half of Christians worldwide attend a
Small Church...* – Church attendance numbers are notoriously fuzzy,
since there is no central authority for tabulating them. And there
are so many issues involved, including what constitutes an "official"
church. When I use stats I will note when they come from a reliable
single source. For the rest, I will use a combination of research,
experience and some guesstimates. But I'll always try to stay on the
conservative side of the numbers for credibility.

Page 43: *I finally gave up looking and decided to write it myself...*
– Since writing this I have found a handful of books that are
specifically aimed at such encouragement. But not enough to negate
the need for this one.

Page 46: *...the "greater things" Jesus promised we would do.* – John
14:12

Page 46: *"If the foot should say, 'Because I am not a hand, I do not belong to the body,' it would not for that reason cease to be part of the body."* – 1 Corinthians 12:21-22 (also in 12:15-16)

Page 49: ... *the experts have proposed to my friend...* – From a conversation with Rev. Doug Petersen

5. Why We Need Churches of All Sizes

Page 54: ...*85% are smaller than 200.* – Carl F. George, How To Break Church Growth Barriers, pg. 132

Page 54: *"I will build my church"* – Matthew 16:18

Page 55: *"one-half of churchgoers attended churches in the top 10 percent of church size."* – Reggie McNeal, The Present Future, pg 24

Page 56-57: *"Those who attend megachurches are likelier to volunteer less, contribute less financially..."* and the stats that follow are from Enrichment Magazine, Winter 2010, pg 20

6. So What's Wrong with Church Growth?

Page 59: *"with rare exception the 'growth' here was the cannibalization of the smaller membership churches by these emerging superchurches."* – Reggie McNeal, The Present Future, pg 22

Page 60: ... *"rise of the celebrity-status church culture ... demoralized leaders"* – Reggie McNeal, The Present Future, pg 23

Page 62: Soar With Your Strengths, Donald O. Clifton & Paula Nelson, pgs 3-7

Page 63: *Stuart Smalley* – Not to be confused with Gary Smalley, a wonderful therapist and author. Stuart Smalley was a recurring character on Saturday Night Live in the 1990s.

Page 65: *"Churches have more in common by size than by their denomination, tradition, location, age, or any other single isolatable factor."* – Lyle E. Schaller, Activating the Passive Church: Diagnosis and Treatment, pgs 25-26

7. Only In a Small Church

Page 85: *"tumble down shack"* – Dictionary of Pentecostal and Charismatic Movements, pg 36

Page 86: *...a re-emergence of large cathedrals will be met with great suspicion and fear, and justifiably so. A New Small Church grass-roots movement is the only way post-Christian Europe is going to perceive a renewal of Christianity as a genuine spiritual movement, rather than a political strategy.* – This is not just my American opinion. It comes from multiple conversations I have had with ministers throughout Europe.

8. Small Church, Big Vision

Page 92: *"As you know, you go to war with the Army you have. They're not the Army you might want or wish to have at a later time."* – from "The Defense Secretary We Have" by William Kristol, Washington Post, December 15, 2004; Page A33. Said by Secretary Rumsfeld on December 8, 2004.

Page 99: *"I wish the church weren't all about the building."* – Dan Kimball, They Like Jesus But Not the Church, pgs 223-224

Page 100: *"to put a Coca-Cola into the hands of every person on earth."* – The seminar speaker was paraphrasing Ernest Woodruff who bought Coca-Cola in 1919, and whose family would run it for generations. Woodruff is widely quoted as having said his goal for the company was, "To ensure that everyone on Earth drank Coca-Cola as their preferred beverage." This was never Coke's official mission statement, and I am unable to confirm that Woodruff ever said it. What he did say for certain, according to Coca-Cola's website, was that during World War 2 he wanted "to see that every man in uniform gets a bottle of Coca-Cola for 5 cents, wherever he is and whatever it costs the Company." (http://www.thecoca-colacompany.com/heritage/chronicle_symbol_friendship.html). The "into the hands of very person on earth" bromide appears to be a broken-telephone version of Woodruff's WW2 goal.

Page 100: *"Go into all the world and preach the good news to all creation."* – Mark 16:15

Page 101: Info on Rao's restaurant can be found at www.raos.com

Page 105: *"Don't ask yourself what the world needs. Ask yourself what makes you (and your church) come alive, and go do that, because what the world needs is more people (and churches) that have come alive."* – John Eldredge, quoting Gil Bailie in Wild at Heart, pg 200 (parentheses mine)

Page 105: *"Make church a book club with soul."* – Dan Kimball, They Like Jesus but Not the Church, pg 224

Page 105: *"...I think the meetings should be smaller. Every once in a while a big meeting is cool, but not as the norm".* – Dan Kimball, They Like Jesus but Not the Church, pg 220

Page 105: *"Didn't Jesus spend most of his time in smaller settings, ... not when he was in the masses with larger crowds."* – Dan Kimball, They Like Jesus but Not the Church, pg 219

Page 108: *"Come and see."* – John 1:43-46

Page 108: *"Go into all the world and preach the good news to all creation."* – Mark 16:15

Page 111: The quote from Frank Wooden is from an email from him to the author.

9. An Open Letter – To My Fellow Small Church Pastors

Page 115: *Here are some more numbers.* – Yes, I'm aware of the apparent irony here. I'm using large numbers to validate the value of Small Churches. But in this case I believe the numbers do matter because they aren't connected to individual congregations, denominations or pastoral egos. They're about worldwide souls. That has always mattered.

10. God Doesn't Take Attendance

Page 119: *"people count"* quote. – Rick Warren, The Purpose Driven Church, pg 52

Page 121: *As Rick himself would say in his 301 C.L.A.S.S. discipleship curriculum, that's their heart.* – Rick Warren, The Purpose Driven Church, pg 372

Page 124: *...two or three people who have come together in Jesus' name...* – Matthew 18:20

Page 124: *...5,000-plus hungry souls...* – Matthew 14:15-21

Page 124: *... counted the hairs on each of their heads.* – Matthew 10:30

Page 125: *"Pastors and laypersons alike want their church to grow. And ... so does God!"* – Ted Engstrom in the forward of How to Break Church Growth Barriers, by Carl F. George, pg 7

Page 126: *"I will build my church..."* – Matthew 16:18

11. A New Way to Define Success

Page 131: *"In the United States, numbers impress us. ...We measure churches by how many members they boast. ... Jesus questioned the authenticity of this kind of record-keeping."* – Francis Chan, Crazy Love, pg 66

Page 133: *"We should measure success not merely by the size of our church ... but also by the depth and quality of spiritual growth in people's lives."* – David Kinnaman, UNChristian, pg 83

Page 133: *"the spiritual instinct of the children of God."* – Helmut Thielicke, A Little Exercise for Young Theologians, pg 26

Page 134: *..." does not take more seriously the objections of the ordinary washerwoman ... this skepticism is by no means naïve."* – Helmut Thielicke, A Little Exercise for Young Theologians, pg 4

Page 135: *"Every tree that does not bear good fruit is cut down and thrown into the fire. Thus, by their fruit you will recognize them."* – Matthew 7:19-20 (emphasis mine)

Page 135: *...when Jesus cursed the fig tree...* – Matthew 21 & Mark 11

Page 136: *"I will build my church."* – Matthew 16:18

Page 138: *... "ran on foot from all the towns and got there ahead of them."* – Mark 6:33

Page 138: *... Jesus abruptly stopped the conversation and healed the boy to avoid a crowd that was beginning to gather.* – "When Jesus saw that a crowd was running to the scene, he rebuked the evil spirit. 'You deaf and mute spirit,' he said, 'I command you, come out of him and never enter him again.'" – Mark 9:25

Page 139: *"You do not want to leave too, do you?"* – John 6:66-67

Page 142: *...he chose the town of Lake Forest to plant Saddleback Church because he had studied demographics to find out where the next waves of population growth were going to happen...* – Rick Warren, The Purpose Driven Church, pg. 34

Page 143: ... *"eagerly desire the greater gifts."* – 1 Corinthians 12:31

Page 144: ...*the Jerusalem Council...* – Acts 15

Page 144: ...on the day of Pentecost ... there were 3,000 added.... – Acts 2:9-10

Page 144: ... *"two or three"...* – Matthew 18:20

Page 145: *"Didn't it belong to you before it was sold? And after it was sold, wasn't the money at your disposal?"* – Acts 5:4

Page 146: *"We take the latest marketing methods, the newest business management fad, and we apply it to ministry"* with the end result that, by Eldredge's reckoning, *"it removes any real conversation with God."* – John Eldredge, Wild at Heart, pg 200

Page 147: *"I don't like institutionalized anything."* – Donald Miller, Blue Like Jazz, pg 129

Page 147: *"There is nothing relevant about Christian spirituality."* – Donald Miller, Blue Like Jazz, pg 121

12. Stages in the Emotional Life of the Small Church Pastor

(no notes)

13. What Do Small Church Pastors Want and Need?

Page 160: ... *"if thirteen people joined up with us, and that was all it ever was, that would be okay."* – Rob Bell, Velvet Elvis, pg 96

Page 160: ... *"all we cared about was trying to teach and live the way of Jesus."* – Rob Bell, Velvet Elvis, pg 101

Page 163: *"For everyone who has will be given more, and he will have an abundance. Whoever does not have, even what he has will be taken from him."* – Malcolm Gladwell, Outliers. Chapter One, The Matthew Effect

14. Just One City

Page 170: *"I have learned the secret of being content in any and every situation..."* – Philippians 4:12

Page 170: ... *"great gain"*... – 1 Timothy 6:6

Page 171: ...*loving relationships? Wouldn't that be a better way for them to know we are Christ's followers...* – John 13:34-35

15. Becoming an Ex-Grasshopper

Page 175: ...*since Adam and Eve sewed fig leaves together and hid among the trees...* – Genesis 3:7-8

Page 180: *"It's much easier to educate a doer that it is to activate a thinker."* – Tweet by @AndyStanley, August 22, 2012

Page 180: *"Doing something right is more important than doing nothing wrong."* – Tweet by @ErwinMcManus, August 18, 2012

Page 180: *"Sometimes the secret to getting things done is just to do them."* – Tweet by @OliverBurkeman, August 10, 2012

Page 180: *"Do or do not. There is no try."* – Yoda, in *Star Wars Episode V: The Empire Strikes Back*

Acknowledgements

There are so many people to thank.

It's been overwhelming trying to come up with an exhaustive list. I guess that's just how it is with a first book. Especially one that's been thirty years in the making.

So instead of thanking everyone and missing just a few, I'll thank just a few and miss a whole lot.

First, thank you Jesus. It starts and ends with you. And because of you it will never end. At least not the good parts.

My family. Shelley, Veronica, Matt & Phil. No matter what happens, being able to lay my head in a home where we love each other unconditionally makes even the bad stuff OK – and the good stuff great. And you too, Sam. Welcome to the family.

Mom and Dad. You gave me, Karen and Kathy the best start anyone could have. And you both read and re-read, lovingly corrected and encouraged me through rough draft after rough draft after rough draft... especially you, Mom (sorry Dad).

Cornerstone Christian Fellowship. What can I say? In 20 years as your pastor we've learned so much together that ten of these books couldn't hold it all. At times none of us knew what we were doing, but we just kept trying. To a large degree this book and the ministry of New Small Church is a tribute to you – and it's my way of telling the world about the amazing church God continues to give me the privilege to serve.

Gary Garcia. You've stood by me for over 20 years as a partner in ministry, growing and learning together. If more pastors had an armor-bearer like you, we'd have a lot more healthy churches. I'm glad I told the board I'd give you a shot.

So many others have read, edited, encouraged and cheered me on through this process. I'm grateful to all of you. If your name isn't on this list, I hope we're still OK. If not, you can write your own book and forget to thank me.

Thank you all,

Karl